Funny Times
presents:

THE BEST OF THE BEST
AMERICAN HUMOR

The Funniest Cartoons, Columns, and Essays
From *The Funny Times* Newspaper

Edited by
Raymond Lesser and Susan Wolpert,
creators of *The Funny Times*

THREE RIVERS PRESS • NEW YORK

Published by Three Rivers Press, New York, New York.
Member of the Crown Publishing Group, a division of Random House, Inc.
www.randomhouse.com

Printed in the United States of America

Design by Karen Minster and Max Werner

Library of Congress Cataloging-in-Publication Data is available upon request.

ISBN 0-609-80919-9

10   9   8   7   6   5   4   3   2   1

FIRST EDITION

Contents

Cartoons by:

Kirk Anderson, Mark Anderson,
Edgar Argo, J. Backderf, Ace Backwords,
Leonard Bailey, Isabella Bannerman,
Lynda Barry, Scott Bateman,
John Baynham, Alison Bechdel,
Jennifer Berman, Meg Biddle,
Ken Brown, Martin Bucella, Clay Butler,
John Callahan, Kerry Callen,
Morgan Caraway, Margie Cherry,
Richard Codor, David Cohen,
Peter Conrad, Lloyd Dangle, Rob Day,
Brad Diller, Nick Driano, Ralph Dunagin,
Tim Eagan, Benita Epstein, Mike Esposito
(Swami Salami), Karen Favreau,
Jules Feiffer, Ken Fisher (Rubin Bolling),
Michael Franzke, Anne Gibbons,
Randy Glasbergen, Ted Goff,
Martha Gradisher, Steve Greenberg,
Bill Griffith, John Grimes, Matt Groening,
Robert Gumpertz, Tim Haggerty,
Peter Hannan, Roger Harris,
Marian Henley, Buddy Hickerson,
Russell Hodin, Nicole Hollander,
Judy Horacek, Constance Houck,
Gary Huck, Sandy Huffaker, Scott Jenkins,
Phillip Jewell, Gunner Johnson, John Jonik,
James Kasmir, Gary Kell, Mike Konopacki,
L.J. Kopf, Peter Kuper, Tuli Kupferberg,

Harrison Lamb, David Langton,
Raymond Larrett (Norman Dog),
Julie Larson, Glen Lash, Mary Lawton,
Carol Lay, Philip LeVine, Thomas Lenon,
Rosemary Lewis, Stan Mack,
Michael Marland, A.C. Marsh,
Scott Masear, Paul Mavrides,
Heather McAdams, Til Mette,
Jim Middleton, Steve Moore, P.S. Mueller,
Tony Murphy, Paul Nicoloff (Blue),
James T. Norman, Nina Paley,
Mark Parisi, Harvey Pekar,
Dan Perkins (Tom Tomorrow),
Rina Piccolo, Dan Piraro (Bizarro),
Jim Pollock, Kevin Pope, Ted Rall,
Libby Reid, Steve Riehm,
Charlie Rodrigues, Flash Rosenberg,
Leigh Rubin (Rubes), Harley Schwadron,
Jim Siergey, Carol Simpson,
Andrew Singer, Mickey Siporin,
David Sipress, Paul Soderblom,
Nathan Stephens, Mark Stivers,
Chris Suddick, Tom Swick, Tom Toles,
Andrew Toos, Brad Veley, Jim Wagner,
Dan Wasserman, Malcolm Wells,
Shannon Wheeler, Kenneth Wickerham,
John Wise, John Wright, Matt Wuerker,
Christopher Zell, Mark Ziemann

An Introduction

Much of the humor we are exposed to in the mass media is mean, cynical, and derogatory. But at *Funny Times*, we specialize in humor that enlightens. We want you, our readers, to be uplifted and empowered with laughter. We want you to use *Funny Times* as a place to rest and rejuvenate from the insanities of the day, and to get ideas on how to face the craziness that's out there with a smile of recognition, instead of a scream of fright.

As editors, we are truly blessed. Every month the most fantastic comedy minds of our generation send us packets of their newest material. We get to lounge on the couch in our office and sift through all these wonderful laughs and insights, looking for the best of the best American humor, the funniest stuff from the funniest minds in the funniest country on earth.

Each month, from this wealth of material, we distill a tabloid newspaper that highlights the humor of the most recent news and political foibles, media fixations, and modern madness. Our contributors come from many different areas of the American humor scene: comedy writers, stand-up comedians, editorial cartoonists, alternative newspaper cartoonists, columnists, poets, novelists, artists, musicians, actors, and even politicians. Some are famous names you'll recognize, while others you'll never have heard of unless you've needed their unique services (such as our prison psychologist in Florida, or our English teacher in Prague). What all our contributors have in common is the ability to make people laugh, and the willingness to share their gifts with the readers of *Funny Times*.

Ray's mom once said, "You can do anything you set your mind to. So why do you want to be a humor writer?" The truth is, we can think of nothing better to do in the world than to make people laugh. ***The Best of the Best American Humor*** is filled with the goods that make us laugh again and again, the cream of the crop, our favorite stories and cartoons from years of *Funny Times*. After you see these pieces, we think they'll become some of your favorites too. If you're tempted to photocopy a few to stick on your refrigerator, or send to friends, we won't mind. All we want is for everybody to know about *Funny Times*, so we can make the whole world laugh.

We wish to thank all the people who made this book (and our absurdly funny jobs) possible, but especially our contributors, and incredibly dedicated staff. Special kudos go to George Cratcha and Amy Jenkins, who kept us laughing while we all worked, seemingly forever, to make this idea a reality. We also wish to thank Ben & Jerry's for creating Cherry Garcia Ice Cream, which has enabled each of us to buy an entirely new wardrobe of comfortable stretch pants.

Raymond Lesser and
Susan Wolpert, editors

Courtesy, Miami Style

by Dave Barry

I got to thinking about courtesy the other day when a woman hit me with her car. I want to stress that this was totally my fault. I was crossing a street in Miami, in a pedestrian crosswalk, and I saw the woman's car approaching, and like a total idiot, I assumed she would stop. The reason I assumed this — you are going to laugh and laugh — is that there was a stop sign facing her, saying (this is a verbatim quote) "STOP." I don't know what I was thinking. In Miami, it is not customary to stop for stop signs. The thinking in Miami is, if you stop for a stop sign, the other motorists will assume that you are a tourist and therefore unarmed, and they will help themselves to your money and medically valuable organs. For the same reason, Miami drivers do not interpret traffic lights the same way as normal humans do. This is what a traffic light means to a Miami driver:

GREEN: Proceed

YELLOW: Proceed much faster

RED: Proceed while gesturing

So anyway, there I was, Mr. Stupid Head, expecting a Miami motorist to stop for a stop

sign, and the result was that she had to slam on her brakes, and I had to leap backward like a character in a rental movie on rewind, and her car banged into my left knee. I was shaken, but fortunately I remained calm enough to remember what leading medical authorities advise you to do if you are involved in an accident. "Punch the car," they advise. So I did. I punched the car, and I pointed to the stop sign, and, by way of amplification, I yelled, "There's a STOP SIGN!" The woman then rolled down her window and expressed her deep remorse as follows: "DON'T HIT MY (unladylike word) CAR, YOU (very unladylike word)!"

I should have yelled a snappy comeback, such as: "OH YEAH? WELL NOW, IN ADDITION TO MY KNEE, MY HAND HURTS!" But before I could think of anything, she roared away, no doubt hoping to get through the next intersection while the light was still red. The thing is, at the time, I didn't think this incident was in any way remarkable. I had no doubt that people all over America were shouting bad words and coming to blows with each other's cars. It wasn't until two days later that I began thinking that maybe we could all be a little more courteous. What got me thinking this was England. I went there to attend a wedding in a scenic area called Gloucestershire (pronounced "Wooster") near a lovely little town called Chipping Campden (tourism motto "We've got your sheep").

I'm not saying that the English are perfect.

Their electrical fixtures look and function like science fair projects; their plumbing apparently was designed thousands of years before the discovery of water. Also, their television programming is not so great.

The TV in my room got four channels, and one afternoon the programming lineup, I swear, was:

Channel 1: A man talking about problems in the British gelatin industry;

Channel 2: The national championships of an extremely slow-moving game called "snooker" (pronounced "Wooster");

Channel 3: Another man (or possibly the same man) talking about problems in the British gelatin industry; and

Channel 4: A show (this is the one I ended up watching) in which five people were taste-testing various brands of canned beef gravy and ranking them on a scale of 0 through 10.

(Of course, we have bad TV shows too. But thanks to cable, we have infinitely more of them.) My point is that the English aren't better than us in every way. But they are definitely more courteous. It seems as though every time an English person comes even remotely close to being an inconvenience to anybody, he or she says "Sorry!" Often this causes the other person to say "Sorry!" for having been in a position to cause the first person to say "Sorry!" This may trigger reflex cries of "SORRY!" from random passersby, thereby setting off the legendary Chain Reaction of Sorrys, which sometimes does not stop until it reaches Wales. I'm pretty sure that the queen, when she's knighting someone, taps him with her sword and says: "Sorry!"

Wouldn't it be nice if we had more of that spirit here? Wouldn't it be pleasant if we tried a little courtesy, instead of shooting each other over trivial provocations? Wouldn't it be wonderful if, when we irritated each other, we said "Sorry!" and THEN shot each other? At least it would be a start.

In fact, I'm going to start right here and now. I'm going to address the end of my column to the woman who hit me with her car, in case she's reading this: Whoever you are, I am sincerely sorry that I impeded your progress through the stop sign. And I am even MORE sorry that I hit your car with my fist. It should have been a hammer.

Halloween with Dad

by Lynda Barry

It's Halloween night and my brother and I are piling into the front seat of my dad's beat up DeSoto. It's dark and raining and he's gunning the engine. An incredible amount of exhaust shoots out the back.

"You guys in?"

He's taking us out trick or treating. Something he's never done before. It was just some sort of idea that hit him at dinner.

"Lynda man, you're on my cape!"

My brother's living eyeballs stare at me out of his Dracula mask.

"Budge over then, Hogula."

I stare back at him through a Cinderella mask with a bad built-in yellow hairdo.

It's been a tense evening. My parents have been fighting. The kind of fighting that's mostly staring without words. I've seen a ton of horror movies in my life. *The Pit and the Pendulum, House on Haunted Hill*, and the one with the chopped off monster head that looks in your window and moves its lips. But no movie could ever scare me as bad as my parents did when they stopped talking.

I look up and see mom standing on the front porch. My dad leans over me and rolls down the window. "Aw, come on, Audrey! Why don't you come with us?" She turns and walks back into the house.

Dad pops the lighter out of the dash and aims the orange circle at his cigarette. He hits the gas. My brother sits up on his knees. "Where we going, dad?"

"I'm taking you to a place where you are really going to clean up. You kids are going to rack 'em in tonight."

All around us dressed up packs of kids are running everywhere. They're running the dark sidewalks, they're tearing up stairs and lifting bags up to people who lean out of lit doorways with handfuls of candy. My brother and I are going crazy watching them. We want to be outside so bad but my dad just keeps on driving.

We cross Rainer Avenue, head over McClellen and then we're down by the lake. Dad pulls over. The rich people's houses. The ones mom loved to drive by any chance she got. She loved to tell dad "Slow down, slow down!" and then she'd point out which houses she wanted, and which houses she didn't, and which houses had the people inside who did not deserve to live there because they had no taste.

Dad smiles at us and points at the street. "What'd I tell you guys? You're really going to clean up. You should have brought you two

"Maybe a brownie or blueberry muffin, but it'll be hard finding something in gingerbread in your price range."

pillow cases." He smiles, but his eyes look like they're watching us through the same kinds of eye holes our masks have.

"So all you have to do is stay on this street and walk that direction, I'll be waiting up there."

"Dad! Aren't you coming with us?"

"Don't worry." He points through the windshield. "I'll be right up there."

We get out and watch the tail lights of the car get smaller and smaller. Maybe he thought we'd have better luck without him.

My brother socks my arm.

"Come on."

We're in front of a huge house with a long curvy walkway. I feel like I'm in a dream. Me standing alone with my brother in front of a giant house on Halloween night and nobody around anywhere. I push the lighted doorbell and it ding dongs out almost a whole song.

"Dag, these people got long door bells."

The door opens.

"Trick or treat!" My brother holds up his bag. "Trick or Treat!"

A guy smoking a cigarette is holding a big bowl of midget Milky Way bars. For a second I'm thinking "Maybe dad's right. Maybe we will clean up tonight. Maybe the guy is going to dump the whole bowl into our bags." We open our pillow cases and he drops in one each and then the door closes.

My brother looks at me.

"Dag, what a cheapo."

For the rest of the houses it's pretty much the same thing. Long doorbells and midget candy. It's the same candy as we get on our street only now the houses are farther apart and it seems like there are more people faking like they are not home. We're getting tired. My brother takes off his mask.

"This is bunk, man! I want to go home."

"I know, same here."

We can see the red tail lights waiting. We're standing by bushes and I get an idea. "Mike. Hold my bag open for me." I bend down and grab handfuls of leaves.

"What are you doing man?"

"So it will look full."

My brother looks at me. We both know that if we get back in time we can still hit some decent houses. And we both know that our dad is trying, and that counts, and we're not about to blow it for him.

We finish my bag and then start on my brother's. Then we put on our masks, pick up our pillowcases, and tear toward the car.

"You're loyal, eager to please, and willing to work like a dog. You could be a top executive if you didn't bark every time a phone rings."

TOILET TRAINING

"I wasn't going to eat your husband, but then he tripped and fell."

DOG DREAMS...

NATHAN STEPHENS 95

BARK BARK!

Pet Peeves

by Tom Bodett

It's been said that people who keep pets live longer. I hope that means they live longer than their pets. At least longer than my pets. It's a terrible thing to say and I'll probably end up in that circle of doggie hell where all the legless yap dogs go because of it, but I can't help it. I want to wring the necks of both my animals, and I don't know what to do about it.

I've had pets for as long as I can remember, but each of them found some way to die quietly before there were any serious rifts in our relationship. A string of hamsters, stunned birds, and chapped frogs worked in and out of a joyful childhood. Then of course there were the more durable breeds of the canine persuasion.

My folks kept wonderful dogs, the kind of exceptional animals that become part of the family. They could be spoken to in plain English, would fret dutifully when a kid was ill, and put up with all the degradation a houseful of sadistic children could engineer. They were never a problem and are still dearly missed.

Now I have a dog and cat of my very own, and I can't stand either of them. I'm a little torn up about it. The cat, especially, has earned a certain amount of tenure around here – I've had him for ten years. He came into my life as a Christmas gift. (Oh. How nice. You shouldn't have.) I initially named him Shark Bait because that's what I had him figured as, but we soon became fast friends. I was a lonely young bachelor living in an unfamiliar Alaskan town, and having something soft and warm around the place was a real asset. His companionship was welcome, and he was a pretty good cat as far as cats go.

He'd do his business outside, was an accomplished hunter, and could swat the snot out of most dogs that messed with him. I guess what we had was a masculine bond. He tangled with a mink one time and got his face ripped off. I had to send him in an airplane to another town to have it fixed, and it cost me a hundred and fifty dollars. That says a lot about the way I used to feel about him.

After I married, he took to my wife more than me and turned into, well, a cat. Cream and egg yolks. He got bitchy and lazy, and I lost interest. I started thinking of him as a piece of furniture, and I guess I have for a long

Eventually, you've got to decide: which one most deserves to be your best friend?

Pros	Cons	Pros	Cons
Complete and total devotion	Sheds	Charles Kuralt	Commercials
Never critical	Vet bills	Old movies	Laugh-tracks
Never tries to sell you anything	Will let you go ahead with any hare-brained idea you come up with	Requires no house-training	Will never beg you to take it for a walk

time now. At least until he started to lose control of himself. I've never had a piece of furniture make a mess like that before.

I'm sure it's just old age, but I can't forgive him for it. I mean, he's not suffering. He sleeps in his own chair, goes outside when he's good and ready, comes in to eat dinner, then craps on the new rug. It wouldn't be so bad if he'd show some remorse, but instead he lies back in his chair with that "You should have known I was ready to go out" look on his face, the smug little face I once went to great effort to have resecured to his skullcap. I just don't know what to do about it. I have a pest in my house. If he were a rat or a cockroach I would know what to do, but he's not. He's a pet. You can't exterminate pets, you have to murder them. I'm not a murderer.

The situation might not bother me so much if it wasn't compounded by the dog. I'm using the term "dog" pretty loosely. A wheelbarrow full of common garden vegetables would offer just as much companionship on a walk.

He's three years old and a beautiful specimen of a black Lab. All except for one thing. He was born with a head of solid bone. You could say he's a good-natured animal, but that's what they always say about stupid dogs. We have to keep him tied up all the time because he'll follow anything that moves. He's never been in much trouble with the neighbor's chickens or anything, but that's because the chickens can outsmart him. The trouble is

that he's big and scary-looking, and nobody wants a big, scary-looking dog running around without a brain in its head. So he stays tied up, and we give him huge amounts of food for the pleasure of watching him lie in the sun and bark at clouds.

It's driving me crazy. When a terminal patient stops producing brain waves, he's declared legally dead. My dog's EEG is flatter than Kansas, but he's healthy as a horse and happy as a clam. We had him fixed a couple years back to see if he'd calm down and pay attention. All it did was calm him down. Now we have a cabbage on a chain in the front yard that eats its weight in Purina every month. Again, I don't know what to do about it. I harbored some hope for a while that he might redeem himself by eating the cat, but gave that up when I noticed the cat kicks him out of the doghouse whenever he feels like it.

I know I'm responsible for these animals. In fact, I can't stand people who mistreat or abandon their pets just because they've become an inconvenience. It's not their fault they drive me nuts, and it's not their fault they're mine. I can't do them in just because I screwed up. They might have been adopted by someone who likes stupid, lazy pets if I hadn't come along.

I could take them to the pound, but that'd just be letting someone else do the dirty work for me. I suppose if I tried hard enough I could find a benevolent soul to take them off my hands, but I can't bring myself to do it. It'd be like asking someone to take a beating for me. Even if they agreed, I'd feel lousy about it later.

What it boils down to is that I can only hope to outlive them. I look forward to maybe a handful of pet-free years before I take the big sleep myself, the sleep not even the bark of a one-hundred-pound dog could jerk me out of. I've buttered my bread and now I'll just have to eat it.

There's a lesson here someplace but I'm not sure what it is. I'll have to sort it out. I've heard of cats that live for twenty years or more, and as healthy as that dog looks, I'm going to have plenty of time to think about it.

Why I Am a Finn

by Eric Broder

As I watched a recent *60 Minutes* report on Finland and its inhabitants, I thought, "These are my people."

The Finns' dominant national characteristic is melancholia. The *60 Minutes* camera swept over dozens of Finnish faces, each one glummer and more downcast than the last. When the Finns spotted the camera, they quickly and

guiltily looked away. On a Finnish bus, the riders looked as if they were being driven en masse to a community proctology exam. Finns apparently are terrified to have strangers talk to them and God help you if you should try to hug one.

I have no problem with this. What some might consider pathological unfriendliness or squirrely behavior, I consider good manners and letting others have their personal space. I often don't look people in the eye because I've always thought it bold and forward. If someone stares at me as they speak, after a while I think, "Get the hell out of here." It unnerves me. I don't need to be gaped at. Neither do Finns. I like that in a people.

I don't see what's wrong with being perpetually downcast either. It doesn't indicate anything except that you're not a grinning nitwit. I've had people tell me to cheer up when I've been in my best moods. So it doesn't translate to my face. Big deal. Who knows what Finns are thinking? They could be coming up with great stuff as they sit there brooding. The world could use a lot more brooders and a lot fewer dinks going around shooting off their big mouths! Sorry if I got out of hand there.

Neither do I like having strangers attempting to start conversations with me. What earthly benefits could talking to me possibly have for a stranger? One minute they're telling you they like your jacket, the next they're asking what kind of bank accounts you have and how you withdraw your funds. The old withdrawal scam! That's what talking to strangers gets you. And I've had smelly guys sit next to me on the bus and say, "Hey, how you doin'? Ha ha ha ha," or point at my book and say, "Is that a good book? Ha ha ha ha..." You think keeping that kind of conversation going is in your best interest? These are the little chats that begin on the bus and end with you buried in a landfill. So I keep up my forbidding, Finnish demeanor and I don't get bothered.

Here at the office one of our sales executives always gives one of our editors hugs and neck massages. As a Finn, I don't go for this. I'm not physically demonstrative and don't think people ought to be hugging and massaging each other in the workplace. When these two start doing this I groan and scowl at them, causing them in turn to make yet more personal remarks about the tautness of my nether regions. But I say, move to California where they squeeze each other in schools, offices, restaurants – wherever – if you want to do that. You're in Cleveland now, a Finnish-type city if there ever was one.

Even our cat Dizzy is a Finn. Dizzy's an isolated character who's often tense and nervous and runs away if you try to hug her. She sits on the sofa at times looking utterly dejected, or like a sullen teen who's just been caught smoking dope. And she'll bite you if you offend her, which could be at any time, for any reason. But she's often very affectionate – at the proper moments. It doesn't come cheaply. What's the worth of love and affection if that's all you give? You've got to mix the sugar and spice. Dizzy, along with Finns, understands this.

60 Minutes showed that one of the ways the Finns cut loose is by getting together and tangoing. The dancers looked as I did when I went to dancing school: like they'd just received death sentences. Maybe dancing gloomily isn't the best way to dance, but that's how I dance, so I doubly enjoyed watching the Finns go at it. My heart filled with identification.

I couldn't believe it – a whole country filled with people like me! The notion elated me so that at one point during the broadcast I got up on my feet. Briefly.

Love by Committee

by Stephanie Brush

I'm beginning to notice that when you're a single person, your life is not run by yourself anymore. It is run by a committee.

In my case, my committee consists of several incredibly well-meaning people: my landlord Doris; my friend Judith; my sister Meredith; my ex-boyfriend Richard; my platonic friend Doug; my cousin Mike; my neighbors Cecil and Summer; my mother, my father, my aunts and uncles; there may be more.

If I become interested in a member of the opposite sex, the job of the committee is to vote, and then lobby, either in favor of the person or against him.

It is kind of nice and soothing to have your life run by a committee: You get to make your own decisions. Unless the committee disagrees with you. In which case, the decision of the committee is binding.

I'll now present the case of a certain young man, "Pete," with whom I have a correspondence. The reason that I know Pete at all is because Pete's committee convinced him to write me a letter. Pete's committee consists of his next-door neighbor, Anne. Anne said I seemed OK.

Pete lives in a different state, but he sent me a snapshot of himself (he's nice-looking) and a Polaroid of his cat, Roxie.

Like a fool, I allowed Pete's photograph to sit on the counter. My landlord wandered in one day, behaving ominously "casual." "Who's THAT?" she said, brandishing the picture.

I said it was "Just a Guy." (Big mistake. Doris is a Jewish-Mother-of-Four, and her personal lexicon does not contain the term "Just a Guy.")

I probably would have let Pete's photo sit in a file indefinitely, but my committee sprang into action.

First, my landlord, Doris, invited me into her kitchen. "You must go on a date with this man Pete," she said.

"I don't even KNOW him," I said.

Doris' 11-year-old daughter, Rebecca, leaped onto the situation. "I'm going to handle this," she said. She wrote a letter, in longhand. "Dear Pete," it said. "I am coming to your state to spend Christmas with you. Remember me? I am going to stay in your house. Love, Stephanie."

I read the letter. "I DIDN'T EVEN WRITE THAT," I said.

"You can sign it," Rebecca said.

Then, Rebecca called up my friend Judith (I am not inventing this) and read her the letter. "That sounds good," Judith said. "I think they will have beautiful children."

"I DON'T EVEN KNOW THIS GUY," I screamed.

My committee asked me to leave the room.

Meanwhile, Pete's committee was doing a job on him, seven states away. By this time, I have spoken to Pete on the phone a few times, so in this way we are able to keep tabs on what our committees are up to:

"What do you think about getting together in person?" Pete asked me, tentatively.

"I don't know," I told him. "My committee thinks it's good idea. But I feel a little nervous."

"Me, too," he said.

I asked Pete if his committee liked me.

"So far," he said. "What would you like to have – lunch or dinner?" This was a question of staggering import, so I told him I would have to check with my committee and get back to him. My committee and I conferred for several hours, during which time we discussed whether I was appearing "too forward" by agreeing to meet Pete in person at this point in the relationship. Pete's committee conferred with Pete, also. The consensus was "lunch." But not too soon. Probably some time in February.

This will give Pete and me plenty of time to hyperventilate, gain and lose 25 pounds apiece, consider breaking the lunch date, get married and divorced, grow a few more gray hairs, peek speculatively at each other's photographs, and generally perish slowly but surely from stress as the Big Casual Day in February approaches.

I KNOW. I can hear all you readers out there thinking, "WHAT ARE YOU GOING TO WEAR?"

Why are you asking me? Ask my committee.

11-30

"You'd think the prenuptial agreement would've been settled already."

Art

Mrs. Picasso's refrigerator

©Rob Day

©1995 SHERSEY

AT THE SURREALISTS CONVENTION

KOPF

THE L.A. PERFORMANCE SCENE

(AS DESCRIBED BY GEORGE DICAPRIO)

STORY: HARVEY PEKAR
ART: PAUL MAVRIDES
COPYRIGHT © 1989 HARVEY PEKAR

THE NIGHT AFTER DORI SEDA DIED, I WAS WITH SOME PEOPLE AT THEATER CARNIVALE WHO DO A KIND OF GRAND GUIGNOL. I WAS DOING A LIGHT SHOW USING BRINE SHRIMP AND WORMS. I'D HIT 'EM WITH COLD WATER AND THEY'D MOVE AROUND AND I'D PROJECT 'EM ON A WALL MAGNIFIED. IT BLEW PEOPLE'S MINDS.

THAT NIGHT, I SAW THIS GUY, JOHN, WHO COMES ON AFTER ME, PRACTICING KISSING IN A MIRROR. I WONDERED WHAT WAS GOING ON.

HE COMES ON IN A MERMAID OUTFIT. HIS LEGS WERE IN THE TAIL, SO HE HADDA WALK LIKE THEY WERE TIED.

HE STARTS OUT BY SINGING AN ARIA INTO A TOILET BOWL. HE HAD AN OPERATIC QUALITY VOICE.

LA DON'E MOBILE

THEN, SEE, HE WAS ALSO A VENTRILOQUIST, SO HE THROWS HIS VOICE AND MAKES IT SOUND LIKE THE TOILET BOWL IS SINGING BACK TO HIM, LIKE A DUET.

LA DON'E MOBILE

O.K. NEXT HE HAS A CONVERSATION WITH A VOICE IN THE TOILET THAT HE SAID WAS GOD'S.

NEXT, HE TAKES A PISS IN THE TOILET...

...CATCHES SOME OF THE URINE IN A GLASS AND DRINKS IT.

THEN HE JUMPS INTO THE CROWD AND DEMANDS THAT THE MEN IN THE AUDIENCE KISS HIM.

EVERYONE IS SHRIEKING, YELLING, TRYING TO GET OUT OF THE CLUB. PEOPLE WERE LEAVING THEIR CARS AND RUNNING HOME.

THE PLACE HAD BEEN PACKED, BUT IT WAS HALF EMPTIED OUT. THE OWNER, A SHREWD GUY, FILLED IT UP AGAIN BY SELLING TICKETS TO PEOPLE ON THE SIDEWALK.

AS THE NEW PEOPLE FILED IN, THE ONES WHO'D BEEN THERE YELLED:

DON'T KISS THE MERMAID!!

RUBES Creators Syndicate, Inc.
© 1995 Leigh Rubin!

Christo wraps the neighbor's house, age 9.

M.C. ESCHER SKETCH

© 1995 NORMAN-N-NORMAN

DILLER

"My mother? She's fine, why do you ask?"

Cutting edge art for Republicans

Wisdom Of the Nineties

by George Burns

Well, what'll it be this time? I can talk about my career, I can talk about myself, or I can talk about two minutes.

That wasn't too funny, but it's only ten in the morning, and I don't get funny until around eleven-thirty. By noon I'm a riot. The trouble is, by then I'm on the way to my club, so the only one who gets to hear me is my driver. Yesterday, he was laughing so hard he almost drove us under the back end of one of those heavy iron flatbed trucks. I said, "What the hell are you doing, Conrad?! If I want a convertible, I'll buy one!" That made him laugh some more and he backed into the car behind us. I said "Conrad, for this I don't need you – I could drive myself." More laughter.

I'll have to get a new bumper, but fortunately there was no damage to the other car. The rest of the way to the club, while Conrad was laughing, I was thinking about letting him go, but how can you fire such a good audience? That was one of the reasons I hired him.

The truth is he's a good kid, and I do need him or some other driver because I don't drive anymore. Two years ago, when I had four accidents in one month, something told me that it was time to give it up. Actually, only three of those accidents were my fault. The fourth was the fault of a feeble man who kept assuring me

MAXINE by Marian Henley

> # GEORGE BURNS'S TEN DON'TS FOR A LONG LIFE
>
> • Don't Smoke   • Don't Eat Fats
>
> • Don't Drink   • Don't Overexercise
>
> • Don't Gamble   • Don't Overeat
>
> • Don't Eat Salt   • Don't Undereat
>
> • Don't Eat Sugar   • Don't Play Around
>
> AUTHOR'S NOTE:
> You may not live longer, but it will seem longer.

tennis court and jogging paths, pounding away. Their tongues hanging out, but they're going to prove that they are still as good as ever.

That's one extreme. The other is just as bad, and probably more common. I'm talking about the senior citizens who think that because they are up in years they are not supposed to get out of the rocking chairs. Things they've done all their lives they stop doing. Everything is suddenly too much for them. They're afraid to move, afraid to go anywhere. They are alive, but they're not living.

I don't believe in that. I may have to cut down, but I don't stop. I still walk around my pool every day, but instead of going around it twenty times like I used to, I now go around it ten times. I still do my exercises every morning, but instead of thirty minutes, I've cut that to fifteen minutes. It's the same with sex. I only talk about it half as much as I did five years ago.

As I already told you, I have stopped driving. But that's balanced off by a whole new activity that I've taken up lately — going to doctors. Not that I've never gone to doctors before. I went to a doctor once about some difficulty I was having clearing my throat. When he told me to quit smoking I went to another doctor for a second opinion. This time I was a little more careful. I didn't just pick any doctor, I made sure I went to one who smoked. When I told that one about my throat problem he told me to forget it. I did, and it went away.

Then about seventeen years ago I was attended to by a whole team of doctors. That was when I had to have a triple heart bypass. Fortunately, my team won.

So I have been to doctors, but never like the past year or so. Some weeks I see doctors four or five days in a row, sometimes twice a day. I build my whole schedule around doctor appointments. It's become a way of life. And it's quite exciting. I get to learn all about diseases I'd never heard of, I meet lots of interesting people in waiting rooms, and I have my pulse felt by lots of pretty nurses. It's getting so if I have a day without a doctor's appointment, I feel let down.

that it wouldn't have happened if he hadn't blacked out.

Don't ask me why I insisted on driving a car at the age of ninety-three. No, go ahead and ask me. And while you're at it, ask the Department of Motor Vehicles why they allowed me to drive a car at the age of ninety-three.

I shouldn't have been allowed to drive a car when I was forty-three — or thirty-three. I was a terrible driver. I not only went too fast, but my mind was always on shows and scripts, so I was constantly making left turns when I was signaling right turns. But at least in those days I could see over the steering wheel. By ninety-three it was ridiculous. My car was known as the Phantom Cadillac. People would see it whizzing by and they'd swear there was no driver.

Look, who am I kidding? I kept driving because I couldn't admit to myself that I'd become too old to do it. It's a thing called male pride. There are lots of old codgers around who have it, and lots more who aren't around because they had it. You see them every day — not the ones that aren't still around, the others — they're out on the dance floor flinging their partners around, on the

Joshua Drives to Work

by Bruce Carlson

Hearken unto my voice, all of you, and learn from my misfortune. For I have dallied long over *Good Morning America*, and now I pay the price. Yea, verily, it is rush hour.

And though I falleth upon my steering wheel and weep most piteously, I goeth not forward upon the highway. And lo! There is wailing and gnashing of teeth, for clients do await me at the office, and my boss does curse my name most horribly.

And woe unto us all who do travel through the valley of the shadow of road construction. For yea, verily, I am stopped near the Machine That Makes Pounding Noises For No Reason, and soon the pain in my head is as a spike through my temple.

And the Lord sends signs and portents unto His people. And the signs say "RIGHT LANE CLOSED" and "SLOW TRAFFIC" and "YIELD AHEAD" and "BOY, ARE YOU SCREWED NOW," and yea, verily, His people become like cattle, and moveth ever more slowly unto their doom.

But now the Lord does smiteth me foully, for lo! as I haveth a cellular phone, so my Departmental Supervisor can reach out unto me in all places, and there is no sanctuary from him. And his voice blasts me as with the east wind, and though I do abase myself, and rend my clothes, and beg, yet it is so that I must work late tonight, yea, until my beard grows long.

Indeed, there is much discourse on cellular phones by those all about me. And many words are spoken, and arms waved, and so do the cars weave and reel to and fro, for yea, they do argue mightily with their secretaries, for lo, the quarterly report should have been typed up yesterday, yet it was not. And so they payeth not attention to traffic all about them, and do merge, and change lanes, and tailgate with great rage.

And while they maketh damn sure that report will appeareth before them when they arrive at the office, so it is that I am driven into a bridge abutment.

Yet I look around myself, and so do I see the doom of others. For there are many children who frolic in back seats, and who do cry out with much noise as an angry multitude.

"I'm hungry!" "She is touching me," and "He's sitting on my side!" and "Are we there yet? For pee we must, and mightily."

But woe! Those around me seem blinded, and think, for reasons I know not, that others cannot see them. So it is that they sing most loudly with their radios, and reach deep into the dark and mysterious depths of their noses, and do scratch themselves most foully within the recesses of their pants.

Yet I cannot escape them. For though the Lord calleth me from the mountaintop, I cannot go there, for the exit lane is closed. And there is much grief and consternation, for now I must drive far, yea, unto the undiscovered country, and I cannot turn back before I am well into the land of outlet malls.

But even though I flee the highway, so I am still punished. For stoplights do plague me, and will not become green. And yet the car that lies close to mine makes a most noisome sound.

And lo! Boom chucka chucka boom is heard throughout the land.

But though a hunger has come upon me, yet my time is short. So it is that I must stop and shout mightily into the face of a clown, and abase myself before those who are exceedingly young and of pimply aspect. For I must get breakfast at a drive-through, as I am growing thin and ill-favored.

But soon it comes to pass that I do howl and the hair of my flesh stands up. For my coffee has fallen into my lap, and I am tossed up and down as in a tempest, and there are many foul curses, and lo, I am most grievous sore. For unto my loins there is a great desolation.

And after having suffered these trials and tribulations, I arrive at a parking lot of wide and open aspect, and I fall upon my brother's neck and weep with joy at the sight. Yet as the

Moses of the Left Lane-ites.

hickerson © 1989. Los Angeles Times Syndicate

Lord giveth, so doth He taketh away.

For there are those who parketh crookedly, and do taketh up two spaces with one car, for fear others will smite their doors. And those with vehicles of an unnaturally large aspect, like unto sports utility vehicles, and extra-wide pickups, that are puffed up and bear a multitude of bumper stickers.

These cars are an abomination and a pestilence in my eyes, for they causeth me to park far from all mankind, out in the blasted wilderness, in the unclean lands, yea, even unto the chain link fence.

And so I must walk many leagues, with my briefcase heavy upon me, and the lessons of this day burned into my soul and other parts with letters of fire. Yet I know only one thing is surely true: come end of day, I shall wander about as a sheep who has not a shepherd. For my car will be lost in the wilderness, and hidden unto me, until all others have left for home.

And lo! I will be late again.

The Most Wanted English Teacher in Prague

by Louis Charbonneau

After dropping out of high school at the late age of 19, Phil came up with a great idea for making money with a minimum of work. A resident of New York City, he started drawing welfare using numbers from falsified Social Security cards. He lived it up for about a year, which was how long it took for New York City's bumbling bureaucracy to catch up with Phil's scam. They tried and convicted him, and Phil ended up spending 6 months in a minimum-security county prison.

After that, Phil decided he was fed up with the East Coast and chose to follow Horace Greeley's famous advice by going West. He ended up in Los Angeles, where he worked on an assembly line for lawn mowers. It was a good job with health and dental insurance, paid vacation, etc. A pugnacious type, Phil couldn't resist getting into a fight with a co-worker who had rubbed him the wrong way one time too many, and ended up nearly dead in the hospital with slight but permanent damage to his spine. While it took him several months to recover, Phil was blessed with $600 a month as workmen's compensation for the rest of his life since it was an injury that occurred at his workplace during working hours.

That kind of money doesn't go a long way in Los Angeles, so Phil got the bright idea of leaving the country for a place where $600 a month would carry him comfortably. Since you can't draw workmen's compensation in America while residing outside of the country, Phil had a fake I.D. made for a friend of his with Phil's name, address and Social Security number on it. Every month this friend picks up Phil's check, cashes it, takes a $100 cut and wires the rest to Phil wherever he may happen to be.

When he began roving, Phil decided to try his luck in Ireland. With his distant Irish heritage, Phil thought of this as an opportunity to get in touch with his roots.

He moved to Dublin and found a place in a cheap pension. One night he was drinking in a seedy part of town and got into a brawl with one of the local toughs. The Irish beat him up good, but afterwards Phil ignored his profusely bleeding nose and went back to his table to finish his beer. After a few minutes, he noticed the tough guy keeping an eye on him so he decided to leave. Moving through the dark streets of Dublin, he heard footsteps behind him. He looked over his shoulder and saw two men following him. Phil figured the tough and his buddy wanted to work him over thoroughly. Rather than running away, Phil slowed down and let them catch up to him. When he heard them right behind him, he turned around and slammed his fist with

all his muscle-power into the face of the man behind him.

It turned out they were two completely different people on their way home from a different pub. The man Phil had hit ran away with a broken nose gushing blood all over. Phil rushed home and packed his bags. The next morning he bought a plane ticket to Prague. Someone had told him it was cheap and that "Czechs love Americans there." Phil managed to get out the day before the warrant for his arrest (still valid today) was issued by the Dublin police.

Once he reached Prague, Phil realized he was in good company. In addition to the American businessmen in the city, the expatriate poets, actors, drunkards and failures hanging out with nothing to do but drink (Phil's preferred pastime) provided good company for Phil. The $500 a month kept Phil in pretty good shape for about three weeks, but after that he had to start borrowing money to keep the beers coming. It quickly became clear that he'd need a few more crowns each month to break even.

A friend of his from the Thirsty Dog (an American-run pub frequented by expats from the U.S.) told him about the English teaching business and gave him the number of Vladimir, a private dealer in the English trade.

He met Vladimir in the non-stop wine cellar next to U medvidku where the Narodni trida prostitutes hang out. Everyone, including the working girls, seemed to know Vladimir

there. Vladimir even looked like a pimp with his full length leather coat and fuzzy white scarf. Vladimir bought Phil a beer and got right to the point.

"Do you speak English?" asked Vladimir.

"I'm American," said Phil.

"Yep, yep. Very good," said Vladimir. He clicked his false bottom teeth as he mused over the possibilities. "I think you can begin as lektor at Wednesday at 4 o'clock P.M., I think yes, no?"

"I've never taught before," said Phil, who was worried that Vladimir would ask for a copy of his non-existent diploma. Vladimir clicked his false teeth and considered what Phil said.

"Yep, yep. This is not problem. You are American. You can to speak as American. Czech teacher of English has very bad intonation. My clients want conversation. Grammar is very bored to them. Please to dress nice. I have very important clients. Yep. Yep."

On Wednesday, Phil's first lesson was with a top executive at one of the Czech Republic's largest banks. This executive took an immediate liking to Phil and recommended him to his colleagues. The executive referred to him as

"Can we trade? They only gave me a book."

an "Expert in Business English." His colleagues also liked him and invited him to their cottages for weekend excursions. Phil was always on his best behavior at these events and never got so drunk that he ended up in a fight with one of them. Within three months, Phil was teaching the entire Board of Directors at the bank.

Vladimir considered Phil his star teacher — and all of his students said he was the best English teacher they'd ever had — and began charging his clients higher prices for Phil. Phil's students never complained about the rising prices. Soon Vladimir opened a two-hour class for a group of students in a room at the Red Cross near Florenc. The advertisement that ran in several Prague newspapers described the course thus: "American business expert holding intensive English course."

The class was packed, mostly with 20- to 25-year-old women studying business management. Several of them developed a crush on Phil, who, despite strong body odor and perpetually greasy hair, had a certain rugged charisma and looked like a slightly more psychotic Matt Dillon. Phil never responded to the continuous offers from his students to accompany them to the pub. He was strongly against teacher-student relationships of any kind. He considered it immoral for a teacher to sleep with one of his students.

Phil began going out with a French painter studying in Prague. He moved in with her and paid the rent for both of them. In the mornings, Phil slept or watched Nadine paint. In the afternoon he taught English. In the evenings he and Nadine sat at the Thirsty Dog where he had been crowned the unofficial king.

Phil claimed to love Prague, but he never tried to learn the language. When he held audience at the Thirsty Dog, he would insist that he would spend at least five or six years in Prague. "It is the greatest city on earth," he once said. One day, Phil didn't show up for his lessons at the bank. The next day he failed to show up for his class with the young female business students. A week later, Vladimir went to Phil's apartment. His landlord said that he and Nadine had simply disappeared, probably

"I'm terribly sorry; but you misread our ad... we're looking for a workaholic."

To McDonalds!!!

BERLIN WALL

horacek

to Paris, and that they had taken the Russian TV set with them. As Vladimir drove through Prague that night, he clicked his false teeth over and over as he ruminated on how to replace his best teacher. He decided to try the Globe, a bookstore/cafe always full of aspiring expatriate poets and novelists. At the Globe, it took Vladimir five minutes to convince a young Californian with a bandanna and a goatee to take over Phil's classes.

Coffee

Coffee and
OCCUPATIONAL HAZARDS:

Office worker:

In the morning

After one cup

Novelist:

Upon waking

After a few espressos

BANNERMAN ©7-96

CAMP CAPPUCCINO

A Brief History of Cafe Pessimism

1970s	1980s	1990s
The coffee of doom	The cappuccino of doom	The caffè latte of doom

horacek

ZIPPY   "WORDS OF ENCOURAGEMENT"   BILL GRIFFITH

DONUTS & CHINESE FOOD

DONUTS & CHINESE FOOD

J. GEORGIE'S DONUTS & HAMBURGERS   DONUTS & CHINESE FOOD

'NUF SAID.

NUTS & CHINESE FOOD

COFFEE DONUTS   TERIYAKI & BURGERS

TIP O' TH' PIN TO 9TH & FOLSOM, S.F. CA.!

© 1995 Bill Griffith. World rights reserved. Distributed by King Features Syndicate.

9-8

Workaholism

by Andrei Codrescu

Once upon a time there was a man who liked to do nothing. He would get up whenever he pleased, put on whatever clothes he pleased, and then, after a brief stroll through the verdant groves outside his perch, he would come to his favorite cafe. He would sip his pensive coffee there, glancing now and then at the fresh newspaper neatly folded before him. Much of the morning passed in pleasant reverie out of which there rose now and then a sharply delicious half-thought that would become full when he committed it to paper, something he rarely bothered to do. He was content to just

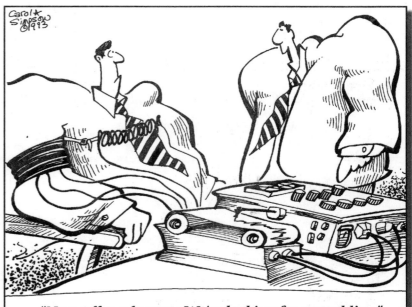

"Now tell a whopper. We're looking for a good liar."

"Dave, would you step out here for a moment? It's time to change your straw and hose down your cubicle."

31

"THANK YOU. I WILL NOW JUGGLE TWELVE CHARTS, AN APPOINTMENT SCHEDULE, THREE NEW GOVERNMENT REGULATIONS AND A BOWLING BALL."

sip at several cups of coffee until it was time for lunch at the house of one or another of his many friends, who were also in the business of doing nothing. During lunch, he would test the thoughts he'd had during breakfast, and was gratified to get several new angles on them. In the afternoon, he would climb onto a grassy knoll and nap, having a number of notable dreams in the process, that would then add themselves to the thoughts born in the A.M. and grown in the P.M.

By evening he was brimming with energy and enthusiasm, and he would go to the bar, where the powerful thoughts he contained would spill forth in explosive abundance between more affluent but less imaginative people. No question about it, doing nothing was what suited him best, although he never had any money to pay either for his coffee or for his beer. But one day, someone bought one of his do-nothing ideas, and asked him for another. After a few weeks, he started to do nothing on purpose; that is, he did nothing deliberately in order to get one of his great (and profitable) do-nothing ideas. He now had enough money to stop doing nothing.

His walk to the café became brisker, less noticing of the verdant brilliance. The coffee was indifferent, and he started actually reading the newspaper he had merely enjoyed for its smell before. Even his friends, instead of conversation companions, became sounding boards. And his dreams got grim and apocalyptic. At the bar, he got into fights. And that's the story of how this man became a workaholic. Instead of doing nothing he was always doing something. If you are like this man, my friend, if you like doing nothing, beware of those who'd pay you for it.

"We've radically increased productivity since we installed the coffeepots."

Romanian Money

By Andrei Codrescu

I'm going to tell you a deep, dark secret. When I was about ten years old, I went to a Pioneer summer camp in the Carpathian Mountains. Pioneers were communist Boy Scouts – we wore little red kerchiefs around our necks and did stuff in the woods.

My father came to visit one weekend. It was the first time I'd seen him in about a year, so I was quite thrilled. We did some father-son stuff like kick a ball for five minutes, and then I watched him smoke. When he finished his cigarettes, he gave me 200 leis and left. Two hundred leis was a lot of money in Romania in those days. An engineer made almost 1,000 leis a month, and engineers made more money than anyone.

The camp had these scary outhouses deep in the woods. After my father left, I had to run to the bathroom. Once there, I realized to my horror that there wasn't any toilet paper. There I was, a young Pioneer in the scary

ECONOMIC/POLITICAL TRUTHS	
Capitalism	Let's sell this shit.
Socialism	This shit belongs to the Government.
Communism	This shit belongs to the People.
Liberalism	Let's spread the shit around.
Conservatism	Keep your hands off my shit.
Clintonism	Looks like shit. Smells like shit. Tastes like shit. Glad I didn't step in it.
Fascism	Eat shit and die.
Totalitarianism	You'll shit when I tell you to shit.
Libertarianism	I'll shit when and where I want to.
Utopianism	I love this shit.
Positivism	My shit doesn't stink.
Separatism	Keep your shit away from my shit.
Ageism	Shit or get off the pot, Grandpa!
Anarchism	Let the shit hit the fan.
Sexism	Clean up this shit, honey.
Feminism	I'm not going to take this shit anymore.
Republican Charity	Who gives a shit?
Perotism	Those other guys don't know shit from Shinola.
Madison Avenueism	This is some really great shit.
Environmentalism	Clean this shit up.
Corporatism	If we merge our shit with your shit, we'll be big shits.

Whew!...thank goodness for the cellular potty!

©1990 Mickey Siporin

Callahan

EMBARRASSING   HUMILIATING   MORTIFYING

DISTRIBUTED BY LEVIN REPRESENTS

Carpathian night with 200 leis in my pocket and no way to clean myself. I was faced with a terrible dilemma: use either my father's money or the red kerchief around my neck, which represented everything communists held most sacred, for toilet paper. It was a confrontation between family and state. It was also a clash between capitalism and communism, the cold war in a nutshell. Father-state, who was everywhere, and father-father, who was nowhere, faced each other suddenly under my distressed bottom.

In the end I chose to use my father's money. There was a practical reason: the worn-out, threadbare bills were better suited for the purpose than the red kerchief. But, in the end, it was a fateful choice. It explains how I feel about many things, money and fathers among them. And now that communism's gone and history has used our red Pioneer's kerchiefs to wipe its problematic self, I get the news from Romania that the government is "recycling the national currency as toilet paper."

"Every week," the report says, "five to six tons of shredded bank notes are sent to a toilet paper factory in Bucharest."

Everything that happens happens because a young boy on a scary toilet seat somewhere makes a critical decision.

Menu Specials

by Cathy Crimmins

Since our generation invented sex, we can't rely on it to make us guilty. But aging requires some sense of morality, and in searching for a new moral scapegoat we have found the perfect substitute: *food.*

It's the new double standard: we take the wholesome foods home to meet the family, all the time longing for the "dirty" fast foods that really excite us. We want grease. We want salt. We want sugar. But we feel terribly guilty every time we scarf down that pint of Ben and Jerry's Heathbar Crunch. We hate ourselves the next morning.

Being DC – Dietarily Correct – is a strain. Friends call friends and confess their strange longings and the gustatory sins they have committed recently. The worst moment is when we're out with friends for lunch or dinner and the waiter asks: "Can I interest anyone in dessert?"

There is a dead silence and then some nervous giggling. The waiter might have asked if anyone was interested in going hunting for spotted owls, or marketing a personal lubricant made out of orca whale blubber.

Everyone looks down at the table. It is the

Baby-Boomers Still Living Dangerously

Not Flossing as a Subversive Activity

by Cathy Crimmins

Hey kids, we're still risk-takers. It's just that the stakes are a bit higher (or lower, depending on how you look at it). Whereas hitchhiking used to give you a rush, or dropping acid from an unknown source was a groove, now we can go crazy in any number of new ways:

- **Drinking caffeinated coffee after 8 p.m.**
- **Ordering the minivan without airbags**
- **Getting a tan**
- **Installing unauthorized software**
- **Throwing away receipts or warranty cards**
- **Not changing the oil filter every 3,000 miles**
- **Buying the generic brand**
- **Ordering dessert**
- **Refinancing the mortgage**
- **Drinking tap water**
- **Not flossing**
- **Sitting in a smoking section**
- **Using latex over oil paint**
- **Canceling your automobile club membership**
- **Bicycling without a helmet**
- **Not getting the three-year extended-service contract on appliances**
- **Having a drink at lunch**

moment of reckoning, and one of two things will happen. Either we will all feel too guilty to say "yes," and there will be a brisk compensatory round of ordering decaffeinated beverages; or one brave soul, looking for another lemming tart to jump off the cliff with him, will ask if anyone else plans to indulge. Perhaps several others will avow that they could manage to *share* one or two pieces of a succulent last course. The waiter will leave and return with several sinful platefuls and thousands of forks. While he is gone, the table will be buzzing with titillating talk of how bad we are being. Once the desserts arrive and consumption begins, everyone will moan and smack their lips in ways that seldom used to be seen outside the bedroom and basically ask each other over and over, "Was it good for you?"

"My modem is opening up a whole new world of opportunities for me—I just told 14 million people to 'go to hell'!"

GLASBERGEN.

THIS MODERN WORLD by TOM TOMORROW

I'M CRUISING DOWN THE *INFORMATION HIGHWAY* IN *HIGH GEAR*...

...RIDING THE *WAVES* OF THE *DIGITAL OCEAN*...

...EXPLORING THE *UNCHARTED REGIONS* OF *CYBERSPACE*!

ACTUALLY YOU'RE SITTING ON YOUR BUTT STARING AT A COMPUTER SCREEN.

AND WHO ASKED *YOU*?

*"Dad, before computers, did you
used to play board games at the office?"*

Darwin Awards

The Darwin Awards are the annual honor given to people who did the gene pool the biggest service by killing themselves in the most extraordinarily stupid ways.

A PAST WINNER:

The Arizona Highway Patrol came upon a pile of smoldering metal embedded into the side of a cliff rising above the road at the apex of a curve. The wreckage resembled the site of an airplane crash, but it was a car. The boys at the lab finally figured out what it was and what had happened.

It seems that this guy somehow got hold of a JATO (Jet Assisted Take Off) unit, which is used to give heavy military transport aircraft an extra push when taking off from short airfields. These are solid fuel rockets which burn as the airplane starts down the runway, then are discarded once the fuel is spent. (They don't have an off switch, but burn until the fuel is gone.) He took the JATO and his Chevy Impala out into the desert, found a long stretch of road, attached the JATO to the car, jumped in, got up some speed, and fired off the rocket. The brakes were completely burned away, apparently from trying to slow the car. The authorities determined that he was doing somewhere between 250–300 mph when he came to that curve.

HONORABLE MENTION:

This man was in an accident and filled out an insurance claim form. The insurance company contacted him and asked for additional information. This was his response:

"I put 'poor planning' as the cause of my accident. You said in your letter that I should explain more fully. I'm an amateur radio operator and on the day of the accident, I was working alone on the top section of my new 80-foot tower. When I had completed my work, I discovered that I had, over the course of many trips up the tower, brought up some 300 pounds of tools and spare hardware. Rather than carry the now unneeded tools down by hand, I decided to lower the items in a small barrel by using a pulley, which was fortunately attached to the gin pole at the top of the tower. Securing the rope at ground level, I went to the top of the tower and loaded the tools and materials into the barrel. Then I went back down and untied the rope, holding it tightly to ensure a slow descent of the barrel. However, I weigh only 155 pounds. Due to my surprise of being suddenly jerked off the ground, I lost my presence of mind and forgot to let go of the rope. Needless to say, I proceeded at a rather rapid rate of speed up the side of the tower. In the vicinity of the 40-foot level, I met the barrel coming down. This explains my fractured skull and broken collarbone. Slowed only slightly, I continued my rapid ascent, not stopping until the fingers of my right hand were two knuckles deep into the pulley. Fortunately, by this time, I had regained my presence of mind and was able to hold onto the rope in spite of my pain. At the same time, however, the barrel of tools hit the ground and the bottom fell out. Devoid of the weight of tools, the barrel now weighed approximately 20 pounds. I therefore began a rapid descent down the side of the tower. In the vicinity of the 40-foot level, I met the barrel coming up. This accounts for the two fractured ankles, and the lacerations on my legs. The encounter with the barrel slowed me down enough to lessen my injuries when I fell onto the pile of tools and, fortunately, only three vertebrae were cracked. However, as I lay there in pain, unable to stand, and watching the empty barrel 80 feet above, I again lost my presence of mind. I let go of the rope and..."

Searching for Day Care

by Donna DeClue

I have a two-year-old boy. He is an active child, an inquisitive child, an energetic child, possibly a wild child. I must work for a living. I must work for my sanity. I must find someone else to care for him. I read ads, make calls, compose a list. He and I will visit each one.

First address: 1450 Kilroy, Boondock City. A woman answers my knock. *"Si?"*

"Hi, I'm the one who called. I'm here about the day care?"

"Si?"

"May we come in?"

She turns to answer someone inside. *"No se."* My son uses her moment of inattention and disappears into the house. I follow him.

I see a family dinner. "I'm sorry I caught you at dinner. Mind if I just look around?" I quickly head off to find the boy. He is in the living room. I pick him off the drapes. The rod's only bent a little, maybe they won't notice.

"Perdóneme, señora, pero..."

"Is this where the children play?" I go out into a beautifully landscaped, fenced backyard.

My two-year-old zips past me and starts caroming around, bouncing off the fence. He sees some flowers. "Mine!" He grabs handfuls of flowers and yanks them, roots and all, from the ground.

I scream, "No, no," and rush to him. He flings the flowers in the air and runs from me, screaming with laughter. I gather the flowers and quickly stuff them back into the ground, hurriedly patting earth around their roots. They lean, but it's the best I can do. The boy is nowhere in sight. The woman has followed us. She has covered her mouth with her hands. Her eyes are wide.

DREYFUS AND I HAVE DISCOVERED A NEW GAME ..... HE HITS ME ON THE HEAD WITH A ROLLED-UP MAGAZINE AND I PRETEND I'M THE BUG HE JUST SQUISHED.

THAT'S PATHETIC.

GRADISHERI...

"We emphasize individualized instruction and parental involvement. Here...you teach him."

I re-enter the house and listen. I hear rapid, excited conversation from the dining room and a crashing sound from deeper in the house. *"Señora, señora?"* I follow the crash to a back bedroom.

My two-year-old is on top of a tall dresser. He got there by pulling the drawers out, stairstep fashion, and climbing up. He pushed a lamp and a jewelry box onto the floor in the process. He is reaching for a low-hanging chandelier in the middle of the room. He leaps. He grabs. He catches. He swings once, twice, three times. He lets go. He flies onto a bed. Whoosh, it is a waterbed. The pillows fly up and onto the floor. As they go, they knock a lamp and a china figurine off the bookshelf headboard onto the floor. Things break. I grab my son. I run. There is yelling.

"Señora, señora? Quien está? Qué quiera?"

My son doesn't want to be held. He holds his arms straight up and becomes slippery. How does he do that? I clutch him tighter and continue to flee. I make a wrong turn. I encounter a swimming pool. My son screams with delight, wriggles free, runs and jumps into the pool. He cannot swim. I dive in and fish him out. He is easier to hold now that we're wet.

We run. We drip. We squish. We find our way out past the astonished-looking people in the dining room and through the living room. The woman who let us in is so excited that I can't understand a word she's saying. My son is kicking around and screaming, saying, "Twimmin', go twimmin'."

We jump in the car. I throw my son in his car seat and burn rubber. As we pass the mailbox, I note the number: 1540 Kilroy. As I straighten the car and accelerate down the street, I look at my note: 1450 Kilroy.

Off in the distance, I hear sirens. Perhaps we'll wait a day or two to make our next visit. Perhaps I'll go alone.

Reprinted from *Dykes to Watch Out For Calendar*, Copyright ©1993 by Alison Bechdel and Firebrand Books, Ithaca, NY.

Drugs

Theism

by Gregory DeClue

My wife is a pantheistic solipsist. A pantheist believes that everything that exists is God. A solipsist believes that nothing exists but oneself. So she believes that she is the only real thing in existence, and that she is God.

I, on the other hand, am a sociobiological existentialist. An existentialist believes that life has no meaning *per se*, but that it is up to each of us to create meaning in our own lives. A sociobiologist believes that humans are a reproductive strategy for passing along genes, and other than what is helpful for survival and reproduction, human consciousness is an epiphenomena; it exists, but has no causal connection to anything. So I believe that it is up to me to create meaning in my life, but it doesn't really amount to a hill of beans what particular meaning it is.

Well, anyway, the sex is good.

When the World Ends, How Will It Be Covered?

by Will Durst

Yo, you know I'm probably not telling you anything you don't already know when I tell you that the newspapers today can be very depressing things to read. What you have mostly are these really smart, educated, pointy-eared brainoid dudes tossing around statistics like "chemical throw weights" and "limited nuclear warfare" and "post hostility squeegeeing," and eventually I think this kind of stuff can begin to wear on your normal average reader. Which is me. Named Designated Normal Average Reader for the nine county Bay Area in the summer of '88, after beating out the other two Normal Average Reader nominees by correctly identifying the names of all the children in the "Hi and Lois" comic strip. (Chip, Trixie and the twins, whose names escape me now but the dog's name is "Dawg.")

Things get uglier in the Middle East every day, so what if, suddenly, without warning (about as sudden as you can get), a world-

wide, five-alarm nuclear holocaust broke out? Wouldn't you be depressed because you weren't able to see how your favorite periodical covered the end of civilization as we know it? Dot and Ditto. The names of the twins in "Hi and Lois." It just came to me. Anyhow, that's where I, Normal Average Reader-man come to the rescue, by presenting a list of the last headlines you are destined not to see.

New York Times: Billions Perish. Bush Calls for Caution.

Golf Digest: Don't Let a Containment Suit 'Nuke' Your Swing.

Life: Parting Shots: The Collection.

Gourmet: Why Not Worms?

Better Homes and Gardens: Rocks: The Forgotten Furniture.

Rolling Stone: The End of Outdoor Concerts?

Motor Trend: Yabba Dabba Doo: The Flintstonemobile Conversion Kit.

Playboy: The Girls of Ground Zero.

Redbook: How to Brighten Your Nuclear Winter With a Bountiful Banquet of Spam.

New York Post: Mideast Missing. Long Islanders Delayed. Knicks Lose Opener.

Fortune: The 50 Best Cemeteries in America for Gold Recoverings.

Vogue: This Fall: Breakthrough in Burlap.

Time: Is Heaven Real?

Newsweek: The Other Side: What Gives?

Architectural Digest: David Letterman's Cave With a View: Mrs. Letterman's Private Tour.

Connoisseur: A New Appreciation for...Water.

Teen Beat: Reincarnation: How Will N'Sync Fare?

Variety: Civilization Slumps. *Rocky VI* on Hold.

GQ: Refugee Chic.

People: Armageddon: Picks and Pans.

Weight Watchers: Learning How to Say YES!

Field and Stream: Are You Man Enough For The 60-lb. 4-Eyed Pike?

Cosmopolitan: 30 Seductive Ways You Can Gain Entrance into a Secure Bunker.

Psychology Today: Departing Means Having to Say You're Sorry.

POSTCARDS FROM AFTER THE APOCALYPSE SERIES

FOR SALE PRIME PROPERTY

The first real estate agent back to the surface

Sports Illustrated: The Greatest Athlete EVER! A Reader's Poll.

Yachting: Tacking into a Mushroom Cloud: A Partial Diary.

National Enquirer: Liz Falls off Diet, New Fiancé Missing.

USA Today: How We'll Die: A Graph.

American Rifleman: Food: The New Weapon.

"THE IRS SAYS IT WILL CONTINUE TO COLLECT TAXES IN THE EVENT OF A NUCLEAR WAR. THAT'S IN CASE THE SURVIVORS THINK THINGS CAN'T GET ANY WORSE."

Car Alarm

by Donna Getzinger

I hear dogs barking outside. Endless Aurf-Aurfing. Who out there really thinks they make the sound "Ruff"? Anyway, they've been barking since two in the morning. What can I do about it? I can't call the police and have them blanket the area with dog muzzles.

This is Los Angeles. Cops have a lot to do here.

I moved to a quieter neighborhood not too long ago. Before, I heard gunshots outside my window intermixed with raped women's screams and crazy homeless people's wailing. I called the police many times back then, but I could never tell them much.

"A woman is screaming outside."

"Can you see her?"

"No. I can't see the street from my window, thank God."

"Does she sound angry or hurt?"

"I don't know. She's screaming. Oh, wait, she stopped."

"Is she okay?"

"I don't know. She just stopped screaming. Maybe she's dead."

"Did you hear anything else?"

"Did I have to? Do I need to have more information to call 911? Have I just wasted your time?"

"We just need the address and your name."

"She was outside. I don't know where." I'd give the address of my building and my name. The switchboard operator always hung up about then. I've never heard a siren within a short time of my report. No operator has ever called back to get more information.

So I moved out of Hollywood. The guilt from that apartment was too much to bear.

Now I hear domestic battles, dogs, and car alarms. Easier on the conscience, harder on the sleep. Gunshots and screams end quickly. Fights and car alarms last all night.

Last night, at midnight, a car alarm was triggered. It was the kind that had four different horrendous sirens that cycle. First there's the

alarm on my old pick-up, and I lost the button thingie that turns it off. One day it got triggered somehow, and eventually it just drained the battery and stopped. At one o'clock in the morning I felt certain the battery on that car would go at any minute.

I was wrong.

At two in the morning I drank warm milk, I read some Joseph Conrad, I used a heating pad on my neck, all things that have always worked toward making me sleepy. None worked because of the constant blaring from outside my window.

As three o'clock neared, my neighbors all around me started talking loudly. They were disturbed too. The apartment below me turned on rock-and-roll music. I never realized how much sound seeped through my floorboards. Suddenly I felt embarrassed. What had they heard me doing down there? I made a vow right then and there to never utter a sound while making love again.

From what I was hearing, no one else was taking steps to actually end the violation of our eardrums. I felt like I had entered that Psych 101 scenario where the girl is screaming on the street but no one in the building does anything to help her. I mean, this wasn't life or death here, but none of us could sleep. Someone had to take responsibility. In my mind, the owner of that car had entered villainhood.

So it was up to me. Everyone else had activities to occupy themselves, keep them from the dreaded call. I did not. I couldn't argue with anyone since I live alone, and I certainly didn't need to play my own music; the tunes

BLAAAAAH one, then the WHOOP WHOOOP one, followed by the LOW HIGH LOW HIGH LOW HIGH one, concluded by the one that sounds like a fire engine WHEE RRR WHEE RRR WHEE RRR. Pretty annoying.

At midnight on a Saturday night it didn't bother me too much. I was just getting into bed, and these things normally get shut off within a half-hour. By one o'clock, on its sixtieth cycle, I was bothered.

I got up and started pacing the floor of my bedroom. How could I sleep with such noise infiltrating my apartment? I didn't think to do anything about it yet. Okay, the owner of the vehicle in question was obviously not around. I guessed that. But, see, I used to have an from downstairs were quite enough. With plenty of chagrin I plodded to the cabinet where I keep the yellow pages and looked up the police non-emergency number listed in the front.

I dialed the number. I was put on hold. On the phone to the police in Los Angeles, I waited on hold for forty-five minutes. I'm not making this up. All I kept thinking was what if I had something important to tell them like I had witnessed a robbery or something. It didn't make me feel real confident. And it wasn't like I had told them my problem and then was put on hold. No. Some computer just kept saying every two minutes or so that the line was busy and it would be answered by the next available operator.

Finally, at four in the morning, someone answered. I really was surprised at that point that the car battery still hadn't died. I figured by the time I actually spoke to someone about it, it would be a moot issue. I told her about the car and that, no, I didn't know where the car was exactly or what it looked like, but I was certain that if a tow truck showed up in

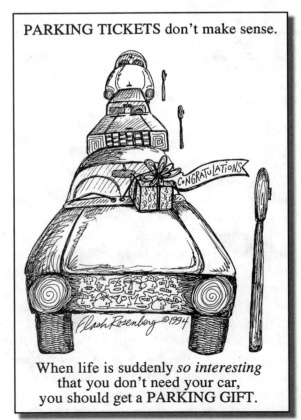

PARKING TICKETS don't make sense.

When life is suddenly *so interesting* that you don't need your car, you should get a PARKING GIFT.

the neighborhood they would hear it. After giving her my address, phone number, and name, against my wishes, I asked her, "Has anyone else called to report this?"

She put me on hold again making me feel guilty for asking. As I used up the phone line some poor gal in Hollywood was probably trying to get through to report a drug deal she witnessed. So I was further irked by the car-alarm villain for making me ruin some unknown person's attempt to do a good deed. After another five minutes the operator came back on the line and said, "No. This is the only report of a car alarm in your area. I'll send someone out there. Call us if the problem continues."

At four-thirty the car alarm stopped. I assume the car was towed or the battery died. Either way, I was pleased. So were my neighbors. A rousing cheer rose up into the early morning air from every bedroom on my block. It was like New Year's. I was the unnamed hero of my neighborhood. I wanted to run out into the street with the neighbors I'd never bothered to talk to before and hug them while breaking bottles of champagne. For the only time in the history of Silverlake, all the residents, every single one of us, were united in feeling. It was worthy of a street parade.

But instead of running out into the street, I put my phone book away, turned out my light and went to bed. At five o'clock in the morning the police called me to ask if the car had been a green Ford Fiesta. I wasn't sure how to respond. Did this mean they hadn't even found the car yet? Did this mean they found it, and they were verifying that I was the witness? Would they tell the owner that it was me who had them towed? Whenever I had reported emergencies or crimes that I was certain were happening, I had expected someone to call me back and say, "You were right," or "The woman is okay. You were very helpful, thank you." But that kind of thing never happened. No payback, ever, for my effort. Last night I was so dumbfounded by this return call from the police that all I could do was tell them to hold while I collected my sleepy thoughts. I hung up and went back to bed.

Environment

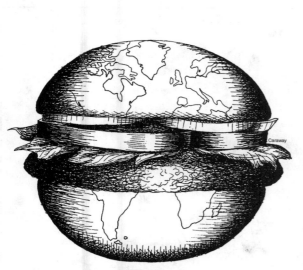

WESTERN MAN'S WORLD VIEW

GLOBAL WARMING FANTASIES THAT WE'RE AFRAID TO CONFESS....

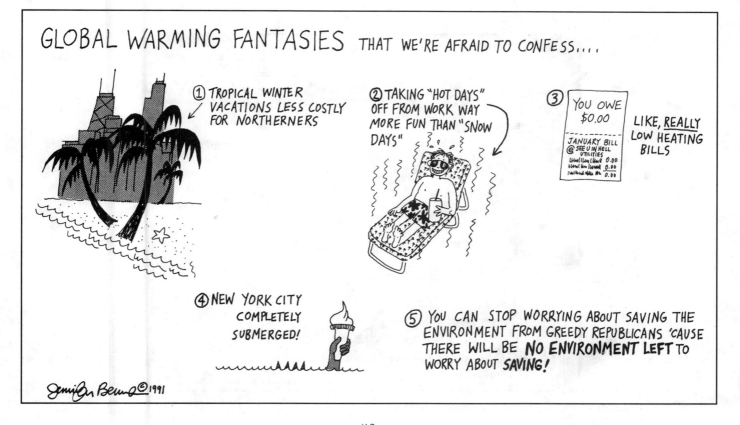

① TROPICAL WINTER VACATIONS LESS COSTLY FOR NORTHERNERS

② TAKING "HOT DAYS" OFF FROM WORK WAY MORE FUN THAN "SNOW DAYS"

③ LIKE, REALLY LOW HEATING BILLS

④ NEW YORK CITY COMPLETELY SUBMERGED!

⑤ YOU CAN STOP WORRYING ABOUT SAVING THE ENVIRONMENT FROM GREEDY REPUBLICANS 'CAUSE THERE WILL BE **NO ENVIRONMENT** LEFT TO WORRY ABOUT **SAVING!**

C'mon, Pigs Of Western Civilization, Eat More Grease

by Allen Ginsberg

Eat Eat more marbled Sirloin more Pork'n gravy!

Lard up the dressing, fry chicken in boiling oil

Carry it dribbling to gray climes, snowed with salt,

Little lambs covered with mint roast in racks surrounded by roast potatoes wet with buttersauce,

Buttered veal medallions in creamy saliva, buttered
beef, by glistening mountains of french fries

Stroganoffs in white hot sour cream, chops soaked
in olive oil, surrounded by olives, salty feta
cheese, followed by Roquefort & Bleu & Stilton
thirsty

for wine, beer Cocacola Fanta Champagne Pepsi
retsina arak whiskey vodka

Agh! Watch out heart attack, pop more angina pills

order a plate of Bratwurst, fried frankfurters,

couple billion Wimpys, McDonald burgers to the
moon & burp!

Salt on those fries! Boil onions & breaded mush-
rooms even zucchini in deep hot Crisco pans

Turkeys die only once, look nice next to tall white
glasses sugarmilk & icecream vanilla balls

Strawberry for sweeter color milkshakes with
hot dogs

Forget greenbeans, every-
day a few carrots,
a mini big spoonful of
salty rice'll do,
make the plate pretty;

throw in some vinegar
pickles, brinysauerkraut
check your cholesterol,
swallow a pill

and order a sugar Cream
donut, pack 2 under
thesize 44 belt

Pass out in the vomito-
rium come back cough
up strands of sandwich
still chewing pastrami at
Katz's delicatessen

Back to central Europe & gobble Kielbasa in Lódz´

swallow salami in Munich with beer, Liverwurst
on pumpernickel in Berlin, greasy cheese in
a 3 star Hotel near Syntagma, on white bread
thick-buttered

Set an example for developing nations, salt, sugar,
animal fat, coffee tobacco Schnapps

Drop dead faster! make room for Chinese
guestworkers with alien soybean curds green
cabbage & rice!

Africans Latins with rice
beans & calabash can stay
thin & crowd in apart-
ments for working class
foodfreaks –

Not like western cuisine
rich in protein cancer
heart attack hypertension
sweat bloated liver
& spleen megaly

Diabetes & stroke –
monuments to
carnivorous civilizations

try murdering Belfast
Bosnia Cypress Ngorno
Karabach Georgia

or mailing love letter bombs in Vienna or setting
houses afire in East Germany – have another
coffee, here's a cigar.

And this is a plate of black forest chocolate cake,
you deserve it.

Ahens, 19 December 1993

GOLD ROOM
WELCOME
HOT DOG
MANUFACTURERS
CONVENTION

©1996 Tribune Media Services, Inc.
All Rights Reserved.

"Marty — come hear what Otto puts in **his** dogs!"

Feiffer®

I SELL TOBACCO.

I'VE GOT BLOOD ON MY HANDS. AND I'M PROUD.

AUTOMOBILES KILL. SHOULD DETROIT FEEL SHAME?

POLLUTANTS KILL. SHOULD THE CHEMICAL COMPANIES SHUT DOWN?

THE ONLY ONE IN THIS COUNTRY WITHOUT BLOOD ON HIS HANDS IS RALPH NADER. AND HE DOESN'T BRING A DIME INTO THE ECONOMY!

IF ALL OF US HEARTLESS, MONEY-GRUBBING C.E.O.s TURNED INTO RALPH NADER TOMORROW— THE COUNTRY WOULD GO BROKE.

CANCER AND HEART DISEASE ARE THE HITS WE TAKE TO KEEP AMERICA COMPETITIVE.

STOP WHINING AND RECOGNIZE THEM FOR WHAT THEY ARE:

FRIENDLY FIRE.

Spalding Gray Goes to Hollywood

by Spalding Gray

Callahan

A.A. IN L.A.

"My name is Mort and I represent Chuck who's an alcoholic."

Just after the earthquake hit Los Angeles, our film, *Swimming to Cambodia*, came out. And if you haven't seen it, you should. You can rent it at your video store. It's a film of a raving, talking head – mine – talking for eighty-seven minutes about some experiences I had while playing a small role in the film *The Killing Fields*. We were very proud of it, but we didn't expect it to do that well – particularly in Los Angeles. It opened when I was out there working on my Monster and it was very popular. And all of a sudden a lot of producers wanted to get in touch with me through my agent. They all wanted to take me out to lunch to find out if I had an idea. There are so few of them going around out there that you can get paid sixty or seventy thousand dollars if you come up with one at lunch. And I thought, all you have to do is drink enough and start talking, and something's bound to come up.

So I told Renee, "I want to take these idea lunches," and I got up to work on the Monster earlier in the morning so I could go out for the idea lunches in the afternoon. I was putting on twenty pounds from those platinum-card lunches that would begin with the bloody marys and the celery – a healthy way to drink – and go on to the sundried tomatoes, and the arugula mache radicchio hot goat cheese salad, and then the poached baby salmon, the dwarf veggies, and the chardonnay, and the fume and the sauvignon blanc, and then the passion fruit mango mousse. And then it's time to talk ideas.

The first person to take me out was a television producer who had read a story of mine. It was a story about Renee and me driving across America and how we ran into a group of retired Americans in the Southwest who called themselves "The Good Samaritans."

What they did was drive around the American Southwest in their Winnebagos, a wagon train of Winnebagos – doing good deeds. And at the end of the day, they would make a kind of wagon train circle around a campfire in a state park and sit out in their folding chairs, drink diet sodas, and tell stories about their good deeds, kind of like Mr. and Mrs. Lone Ranger. Renee and I were taken aboard one of the Winnebagos and given a tour, and I had written a story about it. The producer had read it and wanted to produce a TV series based on it called "The Good Sams." He said, "You could even play Sam."

"Well," I said, "nothing would please me more at this point in my life than to sit by a Hollywood pool and make up television situations. But I don't know how to make anything up. If I could make things up, I'd finish my book. I don't know how to tell the lie that tells the truth – I can only tell what happened to me. I'm cursed with that. But you can send me down there to the American Southwest, and I'll hang out until something happens and then call in my story on a pay phone. That's the most I can promise. But the lunch was wonderful. Thank you very much."

The next to take me out, wine me and give me a big offer was CAA. And if you don't know what CAA is, it is the largest talent agency in the universe, I would say. It's the mafia of talent agencies. It controls the American economy. Look, I don't want to be talking about them tonight. I'd rather not, but I have to because it's part of the monologue. If they ever found out – and I'm sure they already have – that I'm talking about them, I would never work in Hollywood again. And I want to work in Hollywood again because of the health insurance. If you do three weeks' work in a feature film, you get a year's worth of major medical, dental and psychiatric. So there's no way I'm looking that gift horse in any part of its anatomy.

Now listen, when I say they've got them all, I mean it's like a big club. A big power club. And they control all these package deals they put together. They've got all the big directors and all the actors. They've got them all. They've got Bob. They've got Kevin. They've got Dustin. They've got Madonna. They've got Sylvester. They've got Whoopi. They've got them all.

And I thought if they were going to sign me, that might be good for my career, because then I might have a chance to have some power in choosing the kind of role I wanted. And I pictured that I would at last be able to be cast in a kind of forthright, all-American, upstanding, heartfelt, sincere role – where I could at last get rid of my self-deprecating, New York, ironic voice. Really, I saw myself like Jimmy Stewart in a remake of *It's a Wonderful Life* – or certainly Gregory Peck in *To Kill a Mockingbird*, or maybe a new project, *Mr. Spalding Goes to Washington*. But something heartfelt, sincere, all-American, father of three. And I went in there with the intention of being really sincere and decisive.

I walked in and sat down at their big table. There's this round table, a marble table, and they were all there. About ten of them – men and women all suntanned,

windblown and healthy. Oh, so healthy! There are no more drugs in Hollywood. Health is the new drug. Those people have been up since five in the morning doing kung fu, jogging, reading scripts, and eating blue-green algae from the bottom of the Oregon lakes. I'm telling you, I walked in there and they were ready! I have never walked into a room and felt such a sense of readiness in my life. There was nothing happening, but they were ready in case it did. I walked in, and the man at the head of the table offered me the only drug left in Hollywood – a can of Diet Coke. Then he leaned in and said, "Uh, thank you very much for taking time from your busy schedule to come to meet with us. We'd all like to begin by telling you that we all hope you're not one of those artists that's afraid to make money."

And I said, "Um, how much money are we talking about?"

"Well, we did the seventeen million dollar Stallone deal."

"S-s-seventeen? Uh, s-s-seventeen million d-dollars, right? A-all for Sylvester?"

"That's right."

I was conflicted. I didn't know whether to say "Congratulations" or "You should be shot at sunrise." I just hoped that Sylvester had good charities he was giving to.

"And I think if you sign with us today, we could probably make you three million dollars in the next three years. In fact, we could probably start you off tomorrow as an assistant to a Ghostbuster."

And I said, "Well, that wasn't exactly what I was thinking of, but I am — I am flattered. What I'm really curious about is how did you guys find out about me?"

And he said, "We saw your film, *Swimming to Cambodia*, and I never thought I could watch anyone talk for eighty-seven minutes, particularly another man."

"What movie theater did you see it in?"

"We saw it here in the office on tape."

"But it's not out on video yet."

"We have our ways."

"Well, you could do me a favor because my father, um, my father didn't get to see it, because it showed in an art cinema in Providence, Rhode Island, and they didn't have any matinees, and he wouldn't miss cocktail hour."

Then he just reaches around and pulls what looks like a piece of plastic tubing right out from the wall, and speaking into it in a low, devilish voice, says, "Get Spalding Gray's father a copy of *Swimming to Cambodia*, will you please."

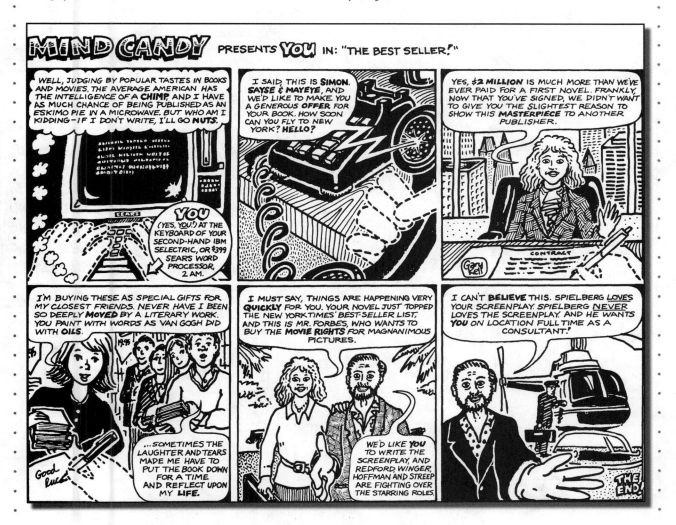

Food

MARTHA GETS THE MUNCHIES

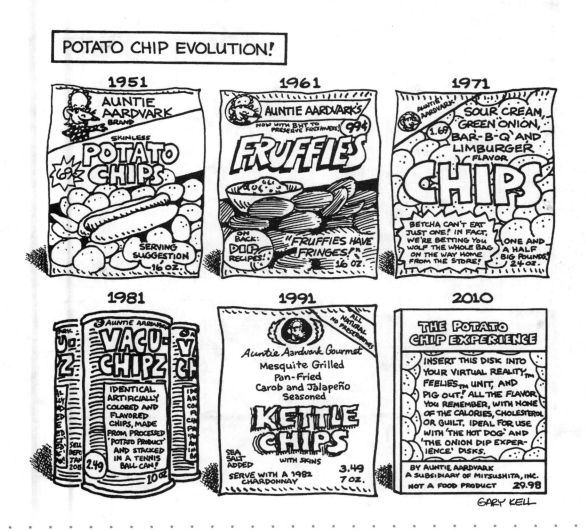

POTATO CHIP EVOLUTION!

GARY KELL

Tom the Dancing Bug

©1991 RUBEN BOLLING

DIST BY QUATERNARY FEATURES

THERE'S BEEN A LOT OF CONFUSION RECENTLY ABOUT MORAL BEHAVIOR. IT'S ACTUALLY A MATTER OF ONE SIMPLE RULE: *THE MORE A LIVING BEING IS LIKE YOU, THE NICER YOU MUST BE TO IT.* CARRY AROUND THIS HANDY CHART, CONSULT IT AS YOU COME ACROSS ORGANISMS, AND ACT ACCORDINGLY.

HUMAN MORALITY MADE SIMPLE

KEY
Y = YES, ALWAYS
S = SOMETIMES, DEPENDING ON CIRCUMSTANCES
M = IF YOU'RE IN THE MOOD
N = NO, NEVER

CATEGORY	EXAMPLE	HOW MUCH LIKE YOU?	APPROPRIATE MORAL RESPONSE	SHOULD YOU HELP IT?	CAN YOU HARM IT?	CAN YOU KILL IT?	CAN YOU EAT IT?
IMMEDIATE FAMILY MEMBERS	DAUGHTER 	ALMOST EXACTLY LIKE YOU	MUST BE UNBELIEVABLY NICE AND GENEROUS. GIVE IT MONEY. DEVOTE YOUR LIFE TO ITS WELL-BEING	Y	N	N	N
EXTENDED FAMILY MEMBERS, FRIENDS	COUSIN 	VERY MUCH LIKE YOU.	MUST BE VERY KIND. HELP IT IF NOT TOO COSTLY TO YOURSELF. MAKE SURE NEVER TO HARM IT.	S	N	N	N
COMMUNITY MEMBERS	FELLOW AMERICAN 	SAME CUSTOMS, VALUE SYSTEM, T.V. SHOWS	MAY ONLY HARM IF YOU CAN GAIN BY IT (EG. IN BUSINESS DEALS). NO NEED TO HELP IT.	M	S	N	N
OUTSIDERS	FOREIGNER 	LOOKS DIFFERENT, ACTS WEIRD	NOTE: THIS LINE NEED NOT BE DRAWN GEOPOLITICALLY ONLY. FOR EXAMPLE, IF YOU VIEW YOUR RACIAL GROUP AS YOUR "COMMUNITY," DROP MEMBERS OF OTHER RACES TO "OUTSIDER" STATUS. CAN BE MEAN TO, IF NECESSARY. MAY KILL, IF WARTIME.	M	S	S	N
PETS AND PRIMATES	DOG 	NOT HUMAN, BUT ANTHROPOMORPHIZED	CAN HARM, IF FOR RESEARCH. CAN PUT IT TO SLEEP, IF NECESSARY. CAN'T EAT IT.	M	S	S	N
OTHER MAMMALS	DEER 	DIFFERENT	CAN KILL, CAN EAT. PAT IT ON THE HEAD.	M	S	Y	Y
OTHER ANIMALS	FISH 	VERY DIFFERENT	CAN KILL, CAN EAT. DON'T PAT IT ON THE HEAD.	N	Y	Y	Y
INVERTEBRATES	LADYBUG	GROSSLY DIFFERENT	STOMP ON IT, FEEL A LITTLE GUILTY.	N	Y	Y	YECH
PLANTS	RADISH 	ABSOLUTELY DIFFERENT	DESTROY WITHOUT A TWINGE OF GUILT.	N	Y	Y	Y

Have Maytag, Will Travel

by Modine Gunch

On a gorgeous Saturday morning, when the sun is shining and the birds are singing and you can smell the flowers, my husband, Lout, always does the same thing. He walks outside and opens up the car hood and leans over and inhales fumes. He clanks around in there for a while, giving us all a view of his buns, and then he goes around and lays down next to the back of the car and oozes under it on his back until just his legs are sticking out. And if you go bend over and ask what is he doing he yells, "Gimme one of them wrenches from the garage. And pass by the kitchen and get me a beer."

After a while he comes inside and gets in the shower and then he lays on the couch. That's his Saturday.

You would think from this that he is taking real good care of this car, so that the slightest little thing that could go wrong with it ain't going to go wrong. His mama thinks that. But I know better. I got to drive that car.

Not that I know much about cars. But I know this. I know that if it is raining and I am in the car and I am getting wet, then this car is leaking. The other day, it is pouring down rain when I come over the bridge and my whole left arm is sopping wet. I get home and I go give Lout a kick where he is lying on the couch and I say, "Look at here. My whole arm is wet." He sits up and he feels my arm and he says, "Did you roll up the window?" Like I am going to drive along in this monsoon, whining about how wet I am getting, but I am not going to roll up the window. Maybe I never got awarded no presidential scholarships or nothing, but what kind of I.Q. does this man think I have? So I say, "Lout, I thought of that. I rolled up the window." And he says to me, perfectly serious, "Are you sure you rolled it up all the way, Modine? Maybe you only rolled it up halfway."

I ain't going to tell you what happened after that.

One time we was having what Lout considers a serious problem with his van. It makes this little clicky sound about once every three blocks. This is a lot worse than a wife with a wet arm, according to Lout. To fix this you got to get up early and make a lot of racket outside so the neighbors will get mad. And if you told your wife you was going to spread fertilizer in the front yard, forget that. Leave that bag of fertilizer by the back door. You got important stuff to do.

So he is doing important stuff and I am sitting on the back steps and thinking about spreading that fertilizer on him, when he comes galloping through the gate. Lout don't never run so this is a surprise. He snatches up the fertilizer bag, throws it on his shoulder, and runs back out the gate with it. I am think-

ing, "Now what? He read my mind?" So I chase after him and when I come around the corner of the house, he is dumping the entire bag into the van motor. Come to find out, something in there caught on fire and he knew not to put water on a oil fire and the only thing he could think to smother it with was the fertilizer. Which is cow manure.

After that, we drive around smelling like a outhouse for Audubon Zoo. It ain't so bad when we first start the motor in the mornings.

But as it heats up, the smell gets stronger. When we pull up to a traffic light people standing at the bus stop start checking the bottoms of their shoes. People in cars roll up their windows. That don't do no good because the smell comes in through the vents. Then they start sniffing their kids. Usually the light changes by that time, so we never get to see the end of all them little dramas we start.

Lout likes motors, but he is not one for cleaning the inside of a van. He says this is the beauty of van ownership. He can fill it up for years before he runs out of room. Beer cans. Old magazines. Carnival beads. He put our old washing machine in there to take to the dump, but then he found out the dump charges for dumping. So that Maytag stayed with us. Wherever we went, it went. It went to Disney World; it went to Dollywood; it went to The City of Snakes and Reptiles.

Then the van gets stolen. From right in front of the house. Lout yells for me to call the police. I grab the phone and then I stop and think. I'm going to report a stolen vehicle with a washing machine and a beer can collection and a smell like a sewer. Finally, I just tell the police it is "loaded with all the extras." And we settle with the insurance people. But at night, I can look up and I know somewhere under that same sky, my Maytag is probably still seeing the world.

DAVID AND DENISE FACED ONE LAST HURDLE BEFORE THE NORGE WAS THEIRS.

The Indy 500: All Alone with a Half-Million Race Fans

by Bob Harris

Last week my buddy Mike the Republican rings me up with tickets to the Indianapolis 500 auto race: tenth-row seats next to the finish line. To a race fan, this is the 50-yard line at the Super Bowl, field boxes at the World Series. So OK, I'll go.

Mike assures me: This is Once in a Lifetime! Thank goodness.

The Indy 500 is the largest single-day sports event on Earth. About a half-million people pour in from every direction, all of them seemingly named "Cooter."

This being capitalism and all, prices for everything are inflated by the sudden excess demand. You want souvenirs? Sweatshirts, only $39.00. White button-downs with A.J. Foyt's name on them, just $47.50. The Super 8 motel, which typically costs $35 a night, charges over $600 for a minimum three-night stay (praise Allah, Mike's boss is paying). This includes – get ready – unlimited use of the Super Toast Bar. Whole wheat with jam? White with marmalade? Rye with butter? Who can decide?

Yeah, well, they don't got this in Minsk, Mike points out.

The race starts at 11 A.M., so the night before I try to leave a wake-up call for 9. The girl at the desk is horrified; didn't I understand that a half-million people would be clogging up the highway? It takes three hours to go ten miles to the track; in fact, most people left wake-up calls for around 5.

We split the difference and get up at 7. True enough, I-465 looked like one of those sci-fi movies where the bomb's about to fall and everyone's brain reboots. If anybody out there thinks Civil Defense was anything more than domestic propaganda, check out a bypass during a holiday weekend. So I hang a right and cut through the city's Section 8 housing, poor

"THIS COMMUNITY HAS BEEN FOUND SAFE FOR THE FOLLOWING RACIAL AND ETHNIC GROUPS..."

neighborhoods where Cooter wouldn't dream of driving. We arrive by 7:30.

A great deal of the "fun" of Indy is the infield scene: tailgate cookouts, beer, touch football in the mud, beer, throwing up, beer... a twin-cam fuel-injected toxic waste incinerating dual-carb gay-bashing culture of macho automotive supremacy. Brotherly love among manly men, where you can high-five or tackle a total stranger. (And that better be all you do.)

Basically, it's Woodstock designed by truckers.

Mike's Jewish. I'm a vegan. The refreshment menu consists entirely of pork: pork hot dogs, pork sausage, pork "Bar-B-Q," etc. I never found the vendor, but several in attendance wandered the infield with oversized Leg of Beast, sort of an all-day sucker for carnivores, large enough for either good eating or giving a beating.

For whatever reason, it's also white as a Klavern. Even later, going over my own race photos and those in the newspapers, I see not a single face darker than George Hamilton in August. Mike begins joking nervously that our fellow spectators may decide on an impromptu game of Jew Toss.

And is this place ever gendered! Women, where they are visible, are dolled up in heavy eyeliner and anti-grav Cosmo girl spandex breast display cases; their primary purpose seems to be the receipt of ongoing requests to "whip 'em out" from half-naked adolescents drunk out of their pods on Old Milwaukee and high-octane testosterone.

Freud would have a field day with the phallic symbolism all over this place. Scoreboards and billboards are unusually long and vertical. For aerodynamic reasons, both the cars and the drivers themselves are arranged phallically, the drivers even wearing oddly-shaped helmets that make their heads resemble, well, um, heads.

At the event's climax, the victor has a ritual drink of white milk, which is always splashed all over his face like the cum shot in a gay porno flick. And before the race, the driver with the fastest car is said to have "the pole."

I'll bet he does.

The pre-race entertainment is a Country Rock show in the infield featuring a big-haired brunette mime-screwing her mic stand while the band plays a bass-heavy cover of "Feel Like Makin' Love."

Fellini-made documentaries.

As for the race itself, it's hard to know who to root for. Cheering arbitrarily as these strangers go around in circles is a bit like watching water go down a drain and rooting for one of the bubbles. Besides, the cars are rolling billboards from Texaco, Copenhagen, Miller Beer, Budweiser, Pennzoil, Player's Ltd., etc. Just pick your favorite public menace and start hollering. You want fuel economy? A big 1.7 miles per gallon.

The drivers are also covered sole-to-crown with dozens of tiny flame-retardant ads, like they walked past an explosion at a Trilateral Commission meeting. I'm surprised they don't charge extra for location – Old Spice on the neck, Speed Stick on the armpits, a big Trojan logo on the crotch, etc.

The cars really aren't even cars at all, but state-of-the-art rolling rockets, Stealth bombers with

training wheels. Actually, the Stealth metaphor is explicit in Miller Beer's TV ads, and the technology overlaps: the Penske racing team is now developing the Racing EyeCue helmet, which uses the same sort of heads-up inside-the-helmet display used on the F-117. But for now, as a Penske spokesman explained, "the idea is to keep the CCM better informed without diverting his attention."

The CCM is the "Car Control Module"– formerly known as the driver.

Eventually, the car's cockpit will be completely enclosed; the improved aerodynamics might allow cars to reach 270 m.p.h. The CCM will be completely dependent on his computers for survival and victory.

Sounds like the military? You bet. All of this technology was pioneered with your tax dollars. Somehow the image of our national wealth squandered so a bunch of rich white boys can race around in circles and occasionally explode in flames seems appropriate.

Somewhere Ronald Reagan is smiling.

And speaking of the spectre of death, it hangs over Indy like the chins over Newt Gingrich's necktie. It's Memorial Day weekend, so the track announcer instructs us to honor those who died in uniform with silence and prayers. Not all those wars were just, but I'm willing to cut dead guys some slack, so I doff the cap. OK. The Archbishop of Indianapolis leads us in prayer, including the weird Samurai-like instruction to "remember the drivers who gave their lives so we may enjoy this race today." Um, OK. Whatever. Again, we pause.

The Father concludes our prayer by pimping his faith for the crowd: "And Lord, don't forget our [NBA] Pacers!"

The moment of silence is forgotten in an instant. Wild cheering. General Chuck Yeager flies overhead in a WWII bomber. The crowd erupts in martial frenzy. Fuck the dead! War is cool! Yeehoo! Red, white and blue balloons are released. Yeager and his boys fly over again. The Purdue marching band plays. Is this a great country, or what?

And they're off...

If you've never been within fifty feet of thirty-three cars doing 250 m.p.h., IT'S LOUDER THAN YOU CAN POSSIBLY IMAGINE. Every animal instinct in my body, five kajillion years of evolution, and a small dollop of common sense all tell me to RUN! PREDATORS WITH SHARPENED TEETH! RUN FOR YOUR LIFE!

Another thing to point out about cars doing 250 m.p.h. is that they are entirely invisible. Poof. Gone. From fifty feet away, your optic nerves — or mine, anyway — can't react in time to follow anything. It's like trying to watch the spokes on a bicycle. This is too much for the tiny lizard part of my brain, which keeps insisting I should RUN! THEY'RE INVISIBLE! THEY'LL EAT YOU NOW! FIND A CAVE! RUN!

All of which lasts precisely ten seconds before the inevitable occurs. Over the cacophony, we hear a much louder noise — a small nuclear event, perhaps? — in the first turn. Stan Fox has lost control of his car and hit the wall head-on at over 200 m.p.h. The nose of his car is destroyed, leaving his legs dangling in the open to be crushed and splintered by passing cars and flying debris.

CAR EXHAUST

SINGER

At anything deserving of the word "sport," the probable death of one of the participants would be considered by the sane as reason to pick up the ball and go home. These large public spectacles are not sports. They are businesses. The participants and spectators are inventory, and nothing more. At Indy, as everyone knows but no one admits, the crashes are the best-selling product.

Unable to see what happened to Stan Fox, we are told about it by one of Mike's co-workers, who was in the area and came to our box, breathless with his story of war:

"Oh, man, we were there! We were right there! This guy like just turned right into the wall and BAM! and this guy T-bones him! It was AWESOME!" After a few minutes of happytalk, the co-worker puts on his wraparound shades and makes for the babes in the infield.

Fortunately, that's all the excitement. Watching the rest of the race is a bit like covering your face with a Handi-Wipe (this is the butt of the person standing on the seat in front of you), turning on a heat lamp, and sitting under a jet engine for three and a half hours.

Jacques Villeeuve of Canada wins when his countryman Scott Goodyear is disqualified for blatant cheating a few laps before the checkered flag. I jokingly attribute the strong Canadian showing to national health care. Mike rolls his eyes.

We head home. Three hours getting out — there are no poor neighborhoods to cut through in the Indy infield — before, exhausted, we watch the reports on the hotel TV while munching on gourmet toast.

The hair and teeth — decked out in checkered ties and earrings (how darling!) — do an Ellis Island on the winner's name, which is rendered by consensus as "Jack Vilnev." The race "highlights" on every channel consist mostly of multiple pictures of Stan Fox, exposed and vulnerable, turning somersaults in slo-mo.

Tut-tut, say the anchors. A real tragedy.

Then, after film of a small plane crash and footage from Bosnia, we see ads from Texaco, Ford, and Miller Beer.

The latest technique for absorbing essential minerals.

Disney just bought your HMO.

"My gosh, the seal *is* broken. I'll get you another pack of cigarettes just to be safe."

A visual look at Alzheimer's.

Waiting: Waiters' True Tales Of Crazed Customers, Murderous Chefs, and Tableside Disasters

compiled by Bruce Griffin Henderson

I once waited on Shelley Winters. She came in with three other people, so there were four of them at the table. This was at Spago. They sat down and they ordered a bottle of wine. It was kind of a cheap bottle of wine. I had just opened and poured it when this rich fan of hers said, "Oh, there's Shelley Winters! Send her over a bottle of wine on me," and he ordered a very expensive bottle of wine. So I went over to them and explained that this gentleman wanted to send a bottle of wine to them. So Shelley Winters says, "Is it good stuff?" and I told her it was really good and went to get it. When I got back to the table she was taking the glasses and pouring the cheaper wine back into the bottle. And you know that's really hard to do with the tiny hole in a wine bottle. She corked it back up and took it home with her. I loved her, she was great.

Another night at Spago I had Shelley Hack at one table, Tonya Roberts at another table, and Cheryl Ladd at yet another table in my station. Three Charlie's Angels who had all played the same part and gotten fired. And they were all talking about one another.

Maryanne Contreras
Los Angeles, California

One time, at Chez Pascal, Susan St. James came in. This was a very expensive restaurant, and we would take the guests' coats and hang them in a cloak room. Well, Susan St. James came in wearing this fabulous sable coat with a matching hat. I took the coat, went into the cloak room, and closed the door behind me. Of course, I immediately tried on the coat and hat. So I'm standing there in this beautiful sable outfit when the door suddenly flies open. Who is at the door? Susan St. James. I was

mortified. She didn't miss a beat; she said, "Are my cigarettes in there?" I reached in the pocket, got her cigarettes out, and gave them to her. She said, "Thank you," and closed the door.

Another time at Chez Pascal, Steven Spielberg came in. He was very quiet and nice. It was a large party, forty people. His people and the people from Atari were celebrating some kind of deal they had just made. It was cocktails and a sit-down dinner. We had a Chateau Margaux we were serving for the first course, which was around $75 a bottle. We went through that, and for the main course we had about the same amount of Chateau Lafite, which was $120 a bottle. I knew we were in trouble; there wasn't enough wine. Sure enough, when the main course was served we filled everyone's glass and we ran out of wine. I went downstairs and told the maitre d' that we were out of wine. He told me that he would come upstairs and knock softly on the wall. When he did this, he wanted me to hand him an empty bottle. So I was taking empty bottles and handing them to him, and he was refilling them with a less expensive wine. We poured the less expensive wine at the table and nobody knew. Customers don't know it, but that kind of shit happens all the time.

I also waited on Madonna. I was working at a place called The Strand, and it was failing miserably. The owner, Sheila, knew tons of celebrities but she wouldn't bank on it. She wouldn't ask them to come in, and when they did come in anyway, she wouldn't tell the press. We were begging her to do it. One day we were empty, and she said a friend of hers was coming in. She said, "I'm really embarrassed, because we're doing so badly." I told her to relax, that her friend would understand. So she's in the back, and Sean Penn and Madonna come in. Then Madonna's family comes in, and the first thing they say is, "We're Madonna's brothers and sisters." They ordered their dinner, and I picked the telephone up and it was Cher. So Cher and Chastity came over with Paul Stanley from Kiss. So we have this loaded table, and I said, "Sheila, call the newspapers." Of course, she wouldn't. And it's a shame, because Sean Penn and Madonna's brother were having a contest; they were pulling each other's hair and trying to see who would scream first. It would have made great copy.

Ted LoRusso
Perretti's, New York City

PERSONALS

I've never seen anything really bad. I guess I have an angel looking over my shoulder. I did see one thing that was sort of a disaster, though. It was in a restaurant where we didn't use trays; we stacked plates along our arms to take them out. And this is sort of a pet peeve, too. Without fail you would be walking by a table with ten plates on each arm and a customer would stop you and ask you for something. Anyway, I was working with this girl who was about to quit her job, and she was walking by this table with about a hundred plates on her arms and they asked her for some ketchup. She looked at them and said, "Sure, let me get that for you," dropped all the plates on the floor at their feet, went and got a bottle of ketchup and said, "Can I bring you anything else at the moment?"

Waiter X
Khin Khao, New York City

I worked at this continental restaurant in Gainesville, Florida. It was Steak Diane tableside, Caesar salad tableside, and a variety of flambé desserts all done at tableside. The waiters at this place started playing jokes on one another; you know how you get bored in a restaurant and you start fooling around. I was waiting on some of my regular customers and they had ordered some kind of flambé dessert—Bananas Foster or Peach Flambé or something. When you make these desserts you flame it with rum, and we were using 85 proof. I got the pan really hot, because the hotter you get the pan the higher the flames leap up. I put a little rum in the pan and it practically exploded. There was this fireball that singed all the hair off my arm and almost lit up this lady's hairdo. I dropped the pan on the floor. I had to. All of a sudden the carpet is on fire and I'm trying to stamp it out and my shoes start to burn. The owner, K.J., came running over with this big pitcher of water and doused my feet and the carpet. The fire was out, but now I'm soaked. It's about 8:30 and I'm going to have to walk around with soggy feet for the rest of the night. I looked around the corner and the other waiters are like Larry, Moe, and Curly, they're just dying laughing. It turns out they had switched 151-proof rum with the 85. It blew up on me! It could have burned the lady's head off. But the worst part was that the other tables in my section were going, "Do it again! We want that dessert!"

Matt Jaroszewicz
Gainesville, Florida

The first month we were open there were three heart attacks and two strokes. I swear to God. Fortunately, the paramedics are right behind the restaurant. We were going to get a direct line. It was amazing, people dropping right and left. It was like, hello, is it the food? It got to where we thought we were going to have to start checking people's pulse rate on

"I'm sorry, sir, the chef, sous chef, two line cooks and the cashier voted not to validate your parking."

the way in, because we didn't need the bad publicity. It's the worst thing in the world when you're waiting on a table and all of a sudden the woman is in her lobster bisque.

Robin Shipley
Granita, Malibu, California

One time at the Warwick Hotel I was waiting on the manager's family. Their food came up and I was carrying it to the table on one of those big trays. Six lobsters, with ramekins full of melted butter and sauce. As I got near the table I felt the tray becoming unbalanced; it was moving slightly forward, and it was going to fall onto the table and all over the man-

ager's family. I had no choice but to go for the wall. So this is what the manager saw me do: I took his family's meal and smashed it into the wall. I lasted another week there.

Ted LoRusso
Perretti's, New York City

When I worked at Benny's Burritos it was always busy and very crowded. We also carried our own banks in bags at our waist. One night this woman was sitting by herself, waiting for a friend, and she had her dry cleaning with her. Her friend shows up and she gets up to greet him and they kind of sandwich me between them. The dry cleaning is in there, and in the confusion she takes my bag, with about $700 in it, and shoots down Avenue A. I ran out the door after her but I lost her in Tompkins Square Park. I called a police car over and I got in the back seat. So we're driving through the park looking for her and they get a call over the radio that a car that people had been selling firearms out of had been spotted nearby. All of a sudden they stop looking for my robber and start chasing this Cadillac. I said, "Guys, I've gotta go back to work," and they said, "We can't let you go right now." The next thing I know we're going over the Brooklyn Bridge and then we're clear out in Brooklyn. They pull this guy over, and I say, "Wait, you guys want to throw me a gun?" These guys had been selling firearms, and I'm

thinking they're going to open fire on the cops. They arrest the guys, and by this time I've been gone from Benny's for at least forty-five minutes. On the way back over the bridge the cops are like, "So what's the food like there?" and I'm saying, "Guys, can we hurry? I've got to get back to work." I walk through the front door and the manager says, "Where the hell were you?" and I just said, "Brooklyn."

Russell Dean Anderson
Miracle Grill, New York City

The most recent disaster we had was a flood. When we had the big rains here, Melrose Avenue flooded over. I looked out the window and the water had risen to the sidewalk level, so there was about two feet of water in the street. I went to the manager and said, "The water is rising," and he looked at me and said, "Well, what do you want me to do about it?" I said, "Nothing, I just thought you might want to be aware that it's on the sidewalk now." About fifteen minutes later it came into the restaurant. People – I'm not lying – put their feet up on the chairs and just hung out and drank their beers. Pretty soon it came all the way back to the kitchen. The whole dining room had about a foot and a half of water in it. Finally we had to turn to people and say, "You know what? We're closing up."

Tom Andonian
Los Angeles

I was waiting on tables during the riots. My roommate and I live in West Hollywood, which was in the middle of the riots, and we both work at Granita, which is in Malibu. The city had imposed a curfew, nobody was supposed to be on the streets. Of course every restaurant in the city was closed except ours. We got letters from Wolfgang Puck giving us permission to drive to work. And the police accepted it because Wolfgang is such a big deal in Los Angeles. So we drove in my roommate's pickup truck to work. We're driving past buildings that are on fire, and nobody is out except for the people who are setting the fires and looting. Our pastry chef is this very strong woman, and she told the restaurant that she wasn't coming in until the riots were over because it was too dangerous. She made a stand; everybody else was kissing butt. So I'm waiting on Shirley MacLaine and it comes time for dessert, and she says, "Where's my crème brûlée? I want a crème brûlée." So I tell her we don't have crème brûlée because the pastry department didn't think it was safe to come to work. I explained the situation pretty thoroughly. And she goes, "What are you talking about? What riots? What do you mean? Oh please, it's not that big of a deal." I was amazed. And on the way home we got shot at. I risked my life to serve pizza to rich people.

Robin Shipley
Granita, Malibu, California

In Daytona Beach there is a big Mexican restaurant right across the street from the Speedway where they hold the Daytona 500. It is a food machine. The menu ran from $5.95 to $12.95. Get them in, and get them out. Every night we'd have a two- to two-and-a-half-hour wait. Every night of the week. And you knew that at 6:45 you were going to be buried. Drugs were encouraged—you've got to keep up with it somehow. Waiters would drink about ten cups of coffee and do a couple of rails and come running out to their tables screaming, "HOW ARE YOU DOING TONIGHT?" One night I got so far behind

"I'll have the Cabernet Sauvignon for my cholesterol, the oysters on the half-shell for my cardiovascular system and the French fries for my inner child."

that I just had to take a break. The tables weren't going anywhere. I'd get to this point where I'd just say, "Screw it, it's chaos, there's no saving this thing, I'm through, I'm not going to make shit off these tables, I'm gonna have a cigarette and drink a cup of coffee." So I'm taking this break and the bookkeeper comes up to me and says, "There's this guy on the phone and I think he's asking for you." I said, "I'm busy right now," and she says, "I think you'd better come and talk to him." I walk over to the bookkeeper's window and I pick up the phone and say, "Hi, it's Matt, can I help you?" and this guy says, "Yeah, I think you're my waiter. I'm sitting down here by this big tree under the stairs and I need some coffee." I just started laughing. I said, "No problem, I'll be right there." So I take the coffee to the guy and fill his cup. A few minutes later he goes to the bathroom and I pick up his cellular phone and get the number off of it. I wait about ten minutes and I go to the pay phone and I call this guy at his table. I say, "Hi. This is Matt, your waiter, you need anything right now?" He about died laughing. He ended up leaving me a tip that was equal to the total of the bill. I had a blast with that guy.

Matt Jaroszewicz
Gainesville, Florida

The Lung-Impaired Liberation Movement

by Molly Ivins

We in the Smoking Community (we prefer to be known as "tobacco co-dependents" or "the lung-impaired" rather than by the tobacconist tag "nicotine addicts") are having terrible self-esteem problems these days. I'm sure all you health fascists are happy to hear this, but I'm warning you right now, our concerns had damn well better be your concerns because we're paying for health-care reform. And don't you forget it. We want respect. We demand gratitude. And we'd also like to have a few planes we could smoke in again.

Our growing list of non-negotiable demands now includes the manufacture and prominent television advertising of a toothpaste that will yellow your teeth. All this white-teeth propaganda you see all over the networks is a threat to our self-esteem. We want affirmative action in the hiring of television characters who will popularize the attractive hacking morning cough.

We want a Smokers' History Week. We demand that schoolchildren be taught the stories of our community's heroes – Bogey and Bette and Duke and FDR. We want schoolchildren (who are currently the victims of so much anti-smoking propaganda that even little ones of 5 or 7 believe they're entitled to tell grown-ups, "Ooo, yuck, that stinks.") taught that politics in this country have gone to hell since the smoke-filled room was declared illegal.

We want it noted that we in the smoking community now spend more time outdoors than the most dedicated environmentalists. We care. We field-strip our butts when in the wilderness and later deposit them in appropriate containers.

The great sociologist of smoking, Susan

Sharlot, has long since irrefutably (more or less) proved our positive impact on society. We smokers are an intense breed: We work hard, we pay incredible sums in taxes, and we die young. We are a net savings to society, particularly in Social Security and Medicaid costs. Kiss our butts.

Of course, we have our extremist fringe: I, myself, oppose the public smoking of bad cigars. But a good cigar, ah, a great cigar is one of the things that makes life worth living – even if it does help life end a little early.

The chewing-tobacco aficionados are, I grant you, an unsightly lot. Nevertheless, the National Pastime would be dead without them and the no-caps-on-salaries provision, so the greater good calls for their continued freedom. Besides, the mouth-cancer specialists need patients.

It's my belief that you health fascists are going about this in entirely the wrong way. Of course, there are people with legitimate reasons to object to smoking. But if you add together all the asthmatics and smoke-allergy sufferers and even throw in people whose nearest and dearest have recently died of a horrible, lingering illness caused by smoking, they're still only a tiny fraction of the populace compared to the Smoking Community. Why not segregate them instead of segregating us? Why not have an asthmatics, allergics and small babies' section in the restaurant?

You may not have considered the fact that the national security is at stake here. I point out to you that Aldrich Ames, the CIA guy who sold out to the Soviets, reports that the reason he was able to pass such a variety of information along to the KGB, on topics far afield from the desk to which he was assigned, was because he picked up the info while standing outside CIA headquarters with other smoking CIA agents. Yes!

Consider as well the cordial exchange of opinion and information among smokers witnessed outside the recent Republican and Democratic state conventions. Democrats talking to Republicans! Liberals talking to Conservatives! Fundamentalists talking to Episcopalians! All of us bound together in the bonds of brotherhood and sisterhood by our mutual oppression as smokers. Standing there, puffing in the rain, our fellowship overcoming the boundaries of such ancient and trifling differences as labor and management, Longhorns and Aggies, bikers and Bach-lovers. (Lung cancer does not discriminate on grounds of race, creed, color or sex.)

We in the Smoking Community, bound together by increasingly cruel forms of segregation, discrimination and tobacconism, are subject to undue stress and alarm. No wonder we need to smoke. I, myself, have been driven to seek medical counsel twice in recent years because of Smokers' Fear; in the first instance, it proved to be a case of pimples on my throat and, in the second, calluses on my vocal cords. (Shows you what a hard worker I am—calluses on my vocal cords.)

I write this to warn y'all of the increasing unrest in the Smoking Community. If you're going to saddle us with the cost of national health insurance, we, by God, want respect and gratitude. That, or we form the Smokers' Liberation Movement.

Rubber Soul

by Frank Johnson

The Roman Catholic Church, my old alma mater, has me worried. A little while ago the Vatican issued a document titled: "Instruction on Respect for Human Life in Its Origins and on the Dignity of Procreation: Replies to Certain Questions of the Day." Fortunately, it was just a pamphlet, rather than a book, which I presume would have called for a full-blown title.

As it is, the document is a pretty thorough condemnation of scientific intervention in the process of human reproduction. Surrogate motherhood, test tube babies, artificial insemination — the essence of these procedures is a separation of the process of reproduction from the act of sexual intercourse, and therefore they are to be banned. In a strange twist, the Vatican seems to be encouraging old-fashioned huff 'n' puff. Saint Paul must be whirling in his grave.

However, according to the Rev. Orville Griese of the Pope John XXIII Center, a Massachusetts biomedical institute in Braintree, some genetic engineering could be tolerated if it were purely therapeutic. This would allow, for instance, routine sperm-testing intended to find the cause of a couple's infertility. All very well and good, I suppose, but the Vatican's manifesto also managed to make this procedure slightly occult by ruling out masturbation as a method of obtaining such sperm.

This presents a rather delicate problem. There are only two ways to obtain spermatozoa as specimen in the doctor's office: 1) masturbation; 2) sleeping nights on the waiting room couch and hoping for a wet dream.

At least that's all I could think of, until I read a *New York Times* article that said Catholic

CALVIN CAUGHT HIS FIRST CONDOM

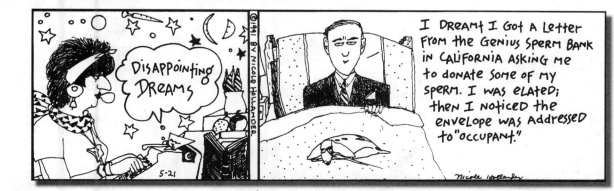

medical authorities have given the nod to a third procedure: "using a condom deliberately pierced with holes to allow some sperm to escape (during intercourse)." Apparently this method would satisfy just about everyone, except those who are sane.

Efficient delivery might be another sticky situation. I suppose the mails are out, given the foolish half-life of the stuff. And special-courier is above and way beyond the call of duty. So I have this picture in my mind of a couple at a doctor's office, bashfully removing themselves to make semi-safe love in a definitely unmissionary position in the broom closet. Finally, triumphant they emerge, carrying the leaky condom, at arm's length, through the reception room. "Sorry about your hair, lady; oops, mister, I guess I got your shoes. Here, use my handkerchief..."

I see this sort of thing happening, but I

Callahan

THE MAN IN THE GREY FLANNEL CONDOM.

Distributed by Levin Represents

guess it's all right because we all must make sacrifices to the gods of theological technology. Of some concern to me, however, is the method for manufacturing a holey rubber in the first place. Should this innocuous little flat tire be created in a factory? In the bedroom? In the garage? With a needle? A nail? If the latter, should it be put on first? No doubt methods will be refined through trial and error. Who would ever have guessed that the lowly prophylactic could be employed as a fertility aid?

Probably not Saint Paul.

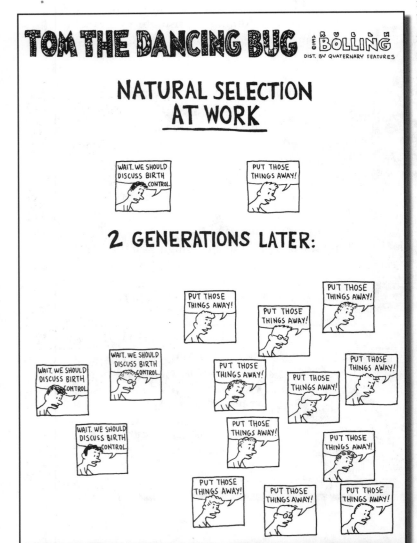

TOM THE DANCING BUG — RUBEN BOLLING
DIST. BY QUATERNARY FEATURES

NATURAL SELECTION AT WORK

WAIT. WE SHOULD DISCUSS BIRTH CONTROL.

PUT THOSE THINGS AWAY!

2 GENERATIONS LATER:

PUT THOSE THINGS AWAY!
PUT THOSE THINGS AWAY!
WAIT. WE SHOULD DISCUSS BIRTH CONTROL.
PUT THOSE THINGS AWAY!
PUT THOSE THINGS AWAY!
WAIT. WE SHOULD DISCUSS BIRTH CONTROL.
PUT THOSE THINGS AWAY!
PUT THOSE THINGS AWAY!
WAIT. WE SHOULD DISCUSS BIRTH CONTROL.
PUT THOSE THINGS AWAY!
PUT THOSE THINGS AWAY!
WAIT. WE SHOULD DISCUSS BIRTH CONTROL.
PUT THOSE THINGS AWAY!
PUT THOSE THINGS AWAY!
PUT THOSE THINGS AWAY!

POPIE TAYLOR

Kids

"GO OVER AND PLAY AT JIMMY'S HOUSE BEFORE HIS MOTHER SENDS JIMMY OVER HERE!"

GEORGE WAGNER

© 1995 Anne Gibbons

@Anne Gibbons

Beverly's life is so hectic, she looks forward to her dental appointment so she can put her feet up.

NINA'S ADVENTURES

©Nina Paley 5-27-'94

YOU MUST HAVE REALLY **LOW SELF-ESTEEM** TO NOT WANT TO HAVE KIDS! WHY ELSE WOULD YOU NOT WANT TO PASS ON YOUR **GENES?**

BECAUSE I'M **NATURE'S FINEST!**

I'M THE END PRODUCT OF **BILLIONS** OF YEARS OF **EVOLUTION!** A BRILLIANT WORK OF **GENETIC ART,** COMPLETED AT LAST! I'M SO **HIGHLY EVOLVED,** NATURE DIDN'T GIVE ME THE URGE TO BREED, 'CUZ I DON'T **NEED** IT — IT'D ALL BE DOWNHILL FROM HERE!

YOU MUST BE AN **EGOMANIAC** TO NOT WANT TO HAVE KIDS!

BEAM!

GLOW!

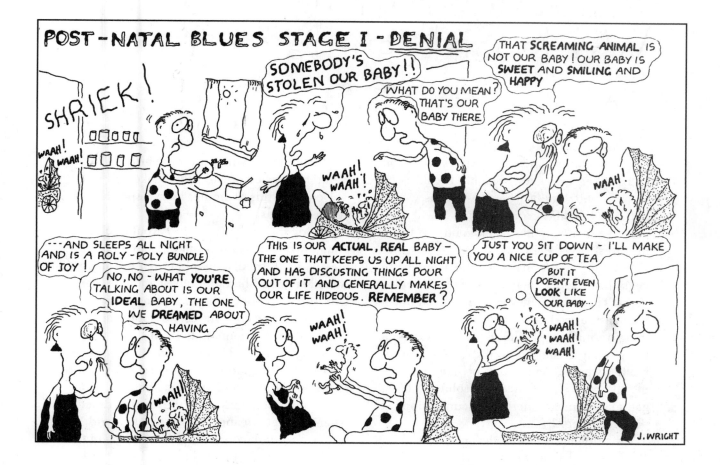

Soul Searching for the Perfect Way to Start Your Day

by Alice Kahn

If you want to know a woman's soul, don't read her tea leaves. Take her breakfast history. Show me a woman who has worked out her breakfast routine and I will show you a woman who has taken control – for 20 minutes.

For me, as for many young women, the years from age 1 to 19 were The Rebellious Years. These were the years when I did not eat breakfast. Breakfast became a symbol of something normal people did. Breakfast was something people ate in books, something my mother wanted me to do to be like those people (although she felt under absolutely no obligation to make personal concessions to normality herself).

Occasionally, in clear view of my mother, I would eat certain select items for breakfast. The white parts of a Hostess cupcake or just the filling in a Twinkie were favorites. These would be washed down with a Coke.

Don't try this at home, kids. Especially if you're my kids.

During the mid-50s, when I would do anything anyone in a clown suit on television told me to do, I tried a number of new sugar-coated cereals. I had the soul of a junkie then. Unfortunately, once the prize was retrieved, I'd had my fix and the cereal soon became tiresome, not to mention disgusting.

In high school, I'd occasionally meet my boyfriend in the morning in the school lunchroom, where the nerds who ate oatmeal (and who would someday rule the world) dined. After a large peanut butter cookie and a furtive peanut-flavored kiss, I had the energy I needed to make it to lunchtime, when it was a hot dog, fries and groping in the cloakroom.

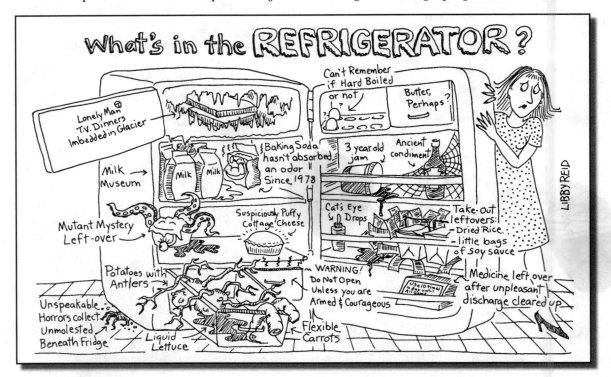

In college, I discovered the egg. Breakfast was the only meal I could ever afford to eat at a restaurant. I felt I was doing something very good for myself when I went out and got the breakfast special around 11:30 — the last possible second you could. Two sunnyside-up eggs, two strips of bacon, hash browns, white toast and jam is what we thought would give you vigor. That was during the Kennedy years when even the Surgeon General probably still smoked a pack a day.

When I got married, I realized that eggs had serious symbolic meaning for my husband. When he was growing up, his budget-minded mother had insisted he eat cereal each day. So, I scrambled for my man and stopped eating breakfast. I was cultivating the lean-and-hungry Lucy Ricardo look.

In the health-obsessed '70s, I went through a wide variety of granolas, hot seven-grain cereals and weird concoctions of natural products from Mother Earth. I liked to start my day with something that looked like a bowl of mud. But my soul was at peace.

I finally settled on Skinner's Raisin Bran. This was the period when I enjoyed the highest illusion of control over my life. I would wake up and smell the herbal tea, see the sun in the heavens, taste the raisin bran in my bowl and feel all was right in the world.

After 12 years of the grand Skinner's illusion, my breakfast world began to fall apart again. Perhaps it was because I became a doubting soul. I questioned whether the raisin bran actually had more calories than I had figured when mixed with 8 ounces of skim milk. And I began to suspect the purity of the product the day a bug flew out of my cereal box. Suddenly I was thrust back into wake-up chaos.

After a few years of wandering the breakfast wilderness, experimenting with various combinations of bran cereal and fruit, I have finally settled on one shredded wheat biscuit crumbled over half a sliced banana covered with skim milk in the blue Japanese bowl. It has to be the blue one.

Most days I'll just eat it with a spoon from the old Scandinavian flatware. But when I'm being very, very good to myself, I will use the real silver spoon.

I recently caught a glimpse of a headline in the morning paper: "Attempts to Develop a Healthy Shredded Wheat." Healthy? The implication, of course, would be that this perfect breakfast that I have finally disciplined myself to eat and find comfort in is actually not the wheat treat it's cracked up to be. Had I read the story, I might have learned that the cereal I had been counting on is nothing more than Twinkie filling, daily requirements-wise.

But I closed the paper. I got out the silver spoon. I'm getting too old for any more truth with my breakfast.

A Pre-Musical Agreement

by Madeleine Begun Kane

One afternoon your 10-year-old daughter comes home from school, enthused about learning to play an instrument. Your eyeballs start to throb. Your head begins to pulsate. You ask yourself whether tin ears are passed down from parents to their children. How do you resolve this dissonant dilemma?

Agreement entered into on the _____ day of _____, 20__, by noise-averse Parents and instrument wielding Child.

WHEREAS, Child has expressed an interest in studying the saxophone;

WHEREAS, Parents hate the sax and don't even consider it a real instrument;

WHEREAS, Child argues that playing the sax may lead to the presidency or at least to a shot on late-night TV;

WHEREAS, Parents concede the worthiness of such goals, but remind Child that after three years of piano lessons she didn't even master "Chopsticks" and, anyway, shouldn't Child play something feminine like the flute; and;

WHEREAS, Child's best friend's mother is letting her take up the sax, and if Parents let Child do this one little thing, she promises she will never again crush her cousin's accordion.

NOW, THEREFORE, Parents and Child agree to the following terms:

1. In lieu of studying the sax or the flute, Child shall play the clarinet, which is sort of like the sax but much less annoying. The parties further agree that if Child complies with this contract for a year, she may, if she deems it appropriate, switch to the sax. Parents feel safe in making this concession because Child has never complied with anything for longer than a nanosecond.

2. Parents shall pay all clarinet rental bills. Notwithstanding the foregoing, if Child

Peter Kuper

doesn't practice at least one-half hour per day, the obligation to pay such bills shall revert to Child, who shall pay them out of her allowance, even if it takes the rest of her life. However, Child's duty to practice shall be void when her body temperature exceeds 101 degrees or when Parents are entertaining guests.

3. Practice sessions shall take place in Child's bedroom with the door tightly shut at all times. In the event a Parent is ill or had a bad day at the office, such session shall at Parent's option be canceled or be conducted in the basement tool closet. Child hereby waives any right she may have to claim that closet clarinet practice constitutes child abuse.

4. Phrases like "But I don't wanna practice" are hereby banned. Any utterance of same by Child shall increase her practice time, except in the event of a Parental headache.

5. Child shall not be required to regale relatives with clarinet renditions of "Do Re Mi," "Jingle Bells" or "Mary Had a Little Lamb." Nor shall Child inflict same on guests without the mutual written agreement of all interested parties. If Child does

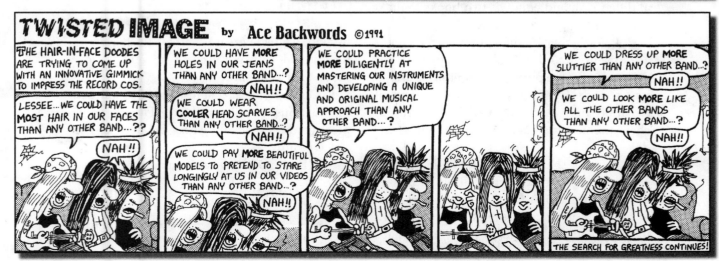

"I hate *Free Baton Night.*"

in fact perform, phrases such as "she's such a cute little talent" shall be strictly prohibited, especially when accompanied by head-patting or cheek-pinching.

6. Child acknowledges that she will have to carry the clarinet to school twice a week for lessons and band practice. The weight of such instrument shall not entitle Child to a ride to or from school. Notwithstanding the foregoing, if Child carries more than four school books on any given day, she shall be given a lift by a Parent to be selected in rotation, provided that Child establishes, to said Parent's satisfaction, that Child used said books within fifteen hours of said ride. Parents concede that Child's arithmetic book is unusually heavy and that it should count as two books in making the aforesaid textbook calculation.

7. Child acknowledges that clarinet reeds are expensive and delicate and agrees to use them only for the purpose of emitting clarinet-type sounds. In return for Parents' agreement to supply her with reeds, Child agrees not to chew them, bend them or feed them to the dog.

8. Parents shall attend Child's band concerts and shall abstain from all embarrassing auditorium activity including but not limited to taking flash photos, jumping up and down in their seats and waving, or yelling, "That's my kid. Isn't she great?" Parents further agree to applaud with enthusiasm no matter how much their ears hurt.

9. Child promises that if she ever becomes a famous musician she will give Parents complete credit, especially when she accepts her first Grammy.

WHEREFORE, we affix our signatures.

_____

_____

Les Miserables

by Margo Kaufman

Why are men such babies when they get sick? My husband has just announced for the third time in twelve minutes that he doesn't feel well. "You married him in sickness and in health," chides an inner voice, so I stop writing and hurry into the living room where he is lying in state on the sofa. "What's wrong, honey?" I ask, bracing for an up-to-the-minute bulletin on his Battle with Disease.

"I have the sniffles," Duke says in the sepulchral whisper used to broadcast golf tournaments and state funerals. He looks up at me with the plaintive stare of a grievously wounded mastiff.

"Oh, no!" I exclaim. This can't be the same man who carefully relocated a rattlesnake from a trail when we were hiking, the man who has his teeth drilled without novocaine. My maternal instincts are immediately inflamed by the absence of machismo. "Let me get you some aspirin," I say. "Do you think that vitamin C would help?" he asks. Actually, I suspect that nothing – and that includes vita-mins, garlic, Contac, or Extra-Strength Excedrin – helps a sick man as much as the knowledge that a busy woman dropped whatever she was doing to go and get it for him. "Lie still," I say. Not that he has the slightest intention of moving. "I'll run to the drugstore."

"It's comforting to have you with your little Florence Nightingale cap on ministering to me," Duke says. With his last ounce of strength he reaches for the remote control and switches on his favorite channel – Channel 18 – where he watches two giant Koreans clad in shorts and garter belts wrestle in a sandbox. I am tempted to remind him that Magic Johnson played in the NBA Championships when he had the flu.

But I know better than to spoil his fun. In my experience, I have discovered that unlike women, men basically enjoy ill health. Still, before I risked the wrath of half the population by putting this in writing, I got some expert opinions.

"When I get sick, I feel great," confesses Glen, thirty-eight, a lawyer. "My God, nobody can expect anything of me when I'm sick. I can just sit around and catch up on magazines and programs I've taped on the VCR, and of course, sleep. And I can also take an Empirin and codeine to make myself feel better without feeling like a drug abuser."

Dr. Alfred Coodley, emeritus clinical professor of psychiatry and behavioral sciences at USC School of Medicine, suggests, "For a certain portion of men, who throughout life have needed to be tough, competent individuals who can deal with everything, illness provides a convenient escape from life. He no longer feels obligated to maintain that defensive, powerful, independent attitude. He has a legit-

"You should blow your nose more often."

imate opportunity to, in a sense, cop out: 'It's OK to be childlike because I'm sick. I'm entitled to be taken care of because I'm sick.'"

"I don't know how I got the sniffles," Duke moans.

"You swam in the ocean on a very cold day," I reply, composing my face into an attentive bedside manner. I know better than to suggest that he sat in a draft. Men like to believe their illness, like a war wound, was honorably gained.

"The water was unusually cold for this time of year," he agrees. Then he gives me a news update: "My sniffles are getting worse." He sneezes once or twice to make sure I get the message.

I get the message. I run into the bathroom and bring him a box of Kleenex. Then I run into the bedroom and bring him a quilt, then a pillow, the television listings, a trash can (used tissues are multiplying on the carpet faster than germs), and a cup of Red Zinger tea. "I'm very grateful," Duke says. "As you know, I have the sniffles."

Of course I know. I wouldn't be this obliging if he were well.

"Getting sick is one of the little tests men have for women," says Rob, thirty-two, a screenwriter. "If a woman doesn't perform well in your sickness, it will never happen."

What's a good performance? "A full mother. My last girlfriend did the right thing. When I had a cold she immediately bought some chicken and made some soup. She even had her own concoction of hot water, lemon juice and honey, which she called Sickee Tea. The important thing about Sickee Tea is that you don't make it yourself, someone has to make it for you."

Robert explains that "a woman who behaves badly is a woman who tells you that when she is sick, she never gives in, she goes out and does anything.

You don't want to hear that a woman is more macho than you. I had a girlfriend who actually said, 'What are you doing in bed? Let's go to a concert.' She didn't understand that I was really kind of enjoying my cold. I thought it was something that we could share together. She didn't see it that way. She thought I was a wimp."

There is a limit to how long even the most understanding woman can cater to a man who lies in a pool of sweat (a man who is too sick to take a shower, but not sick enough to see a doctor) without contemplating euthanasia.

"The only thing you should ever do for a sick man is offer to drive him to the hospital," sneers Claire, an interior designer. "Or drive yourself before he drives you crazy. Fred actually expects me to sit by his side and do anything he wants. There's no use leaving the room — as soon as you do, you'll hear a weak moan that sounds like a request. And I'll say, 'Did you just ask me for a heating pad?' and he'll whimper, 'What? What? Don't make me yell. I'm sick.' Or worse, he'll say things like, 'I'm not hungry but don't you think I should eat something?' which of course means he wants me to make something but he won't tell me what — I'm supposed to guess the magic

"In preparation for cold and flu season I have donned the sneeze-guard hat!"

"WANT TO PLAY PRIMARY HEALTH CARE PROVIDER?"

entire Channel 18 lineup: Farsi lounge acts, Indian music videos, Armenian Teletime, and the weekly Yugoslav show (with its slogan, "From the Adriatic to the Pacific"). "Have you seen my Merck Manual?" he asks.

"No," I lie. Reading a Merck Manual is guaranteed to prolong even the most minor ailment. In case you don't know, the Merck Manual is to bodies what the Chilton Manuals are to cars. It is a hypochondriac's bible, 2,462 pages of small print that details everything you never wanted to know about common, rare, fatal, or merely life-threatening diseases.

Here's what happens when a man gets his hands on a Merck. One Sunday afternoon, Duke cut the grass with a Weed Eater. Half an hour later, I found him poring over his Merck.

"What's the matter?" I asked, alarmed when I noticed that he was reading about multiple sclerosis.

"My hand keeps trembling," Duke said.

"Was it trembling before you mowed the lawn?" I asked. Duke shook his head.

"Then why don't you assume it's vibrating from the Weed Eater?"

"I guess it could be," Duke said, sounding disappointed.

My friend Léon, who swears that "all men are hypochondriacs beyond belief," has never been with a man who didn't have a Merck. But she has learned how to use it to get revenge. She called her boyfriend, who was complaining about "intestinal heaviness," and said, "I'm looking through a medical book and I think I found what's wrong." Then, she says, "I read him about fourteen symptoms to which he eagerly answered, 'Yes, yes.' You would have thought the prize at the end was a Maserati. Then he asked, 'What have I got?' I really enjoyed telling him: 'A tipped uterus.' He hung up the phone. He later complained that I didn't 'take his symptoms seriously.'"

Here's another surefire way to heal a sick man in a hurry:

I trudge slowly into Duke's sickroom. "I don't feel well, honey," I moan. Duke bounds out of bed and throws on his clothes. "Excuse me," he says. "I've got to flush the cooling system in my car."

potion. He's thirty-eight years old. Can you believe it?"

"Maybe it's because men are used to being spoiled by their wives and mothers," speculates Dr. Harry Sperling, an Encino ear, nose, and throat specialist.

"Men can act like babies when they're sick, and that is reinforced by a woman's responses because women are known behaviorally to be more nurturing than men," says Dr. Thomas Lasswell, professor of sociology at the James A. Peterson Human Relations Center at USC.

"My tummy hurts," Duke reports the next day. I am not surprised. He has digested the

Law & Order

THEREFORE MOREOVER, WHEREAS,

LAWYERS ON STRIKE

GOFF

SINGER

"As your lawyer, I must advise you to drop this suit against the dairy industry and get back in your stall."

A Wobegon Holiday Dinner
What happened when the clan sat down to turkey

by Garrison Keillor

"SINCE WE'RE NEW HERE, WOULD YOU MIND IF WE CLEARED THE FOREST BETWEEN OUR ENCAMPMENTS SO WE CAN OBSERVE HOW YOU LIVE IN HARMONY WITH NATURE?"

My cousin Duke called me one day last week when I was in the middle of something, but I swiveled my chair back and put my feet up on the windowsill and we talked for half an hour, which was good. My relatives never call me anymore since I moved to New York because they imagine I'm busy, and when they do call, they say, "Did I catch you at a bad time? Are you busy? You're busy, aren't you? I'm sorry. I didn't mean to bother you. I can call you back later. Sorry. Bye."

This was a more normal conversation. She said it was snowing in Minnesota and was still deer-hunting season, so she was staying indoors and away from windows. She had arrived in Lake Wobegon on Halloween from Seattle where she lives, taking a month's leave to see her mother, my aunt Lois, who is ailing, though you wouldn't know this from talking to my aunt, who is no complainer. "How are you, Mary Ann?" I asked. It's hard to think of her as Mary Ann, having known her as Duke since she was tiny, but she left her Dukedom to become a Mary Ann in Seattle, I guess, and we must honor that.

She said she is thinking of quitting her social worker job. "I'm getting so extremely tired of poor people and their problems," she said, which warmed my heart: A horrible thing like that, you only dare confess to someone you love. "They're angry and sick and abusive, and I don't blame them, I'm just tired of them," she said. This reminded us both of the Halloween when we were small when the powers that be decided that, instead of trick-or-treating, children should go door to door and collect money to give the UNICEF to help little starving children in foreign lands. So we did. We hated it and we despised those starving children for making it necessary. (This experience so embittered my classmates that they later voted Republican, and, in 1981, Mr. Reagan came to Washington to tell America that it's okay to get as many Milky Ways as you want and to keep them all for yourself and that little starving children are really ballet dancers. But I am still a liberal. I keep my Milky Ways but I give licorice whips to the poor.)

She said she was thinking about opening a hardware store for women. She is sick of old hardware guys treating her like a small damp child. The store would have an all-women staff. "If you had a hardware store that wouldn't humiliate people who don't know the names of things, you'd really have a gold mine," she said. She wanted me to invest in it. She said, "We could make it a combination hardware-bookstore. It might work." I'm sure it would. Ten years from now, I'll read somewhere that the hardware-bookstore was the hot idea of the '90s, but I don't care. I bought a New York apartment in 1988 when the market was at its height and now, according to the paper, my apartment has lost 25 percent of its value, and I'm not sure I'm a believer in capitalism anymore.

"Oh well," she said. She was in a good mood. She was sitting in the kitchen of her childhood home, and the sight of snow made her cheerful, but her family was always cheerful. Aunt Lois inherited it from my grandma, who spent her last years baking good bread and whistling and thinking highly of her grandchildren. Duke said, "You know something? This month, it will be 25 years since the last time I vomited."

I asked her how she planned to celebrate the anniversary, and she said she wasn't sure. I said, "I sure remember the event." So did she, vividly. Mary Ann is a slight woman, like Lois, and elegant, even in jeans and a sweatshirt, and she would rather lie very still for days on a couch than throw up. She never rides the Ferris wheel, is leery of airplanes and doesn't drink more than one glass of wine per dinner. Other people in our family, if they feel a little queasy, think nothing of heading for the bathroom and taking matters into their own hands, but Mary Ann would rather lie very still in a dark room with a cold compress on her forehead.

The last time Duke threw up was Thanksgiving Day, 1965. It was the last year our whole family, aunts and uncles and cousins, were together at Al and Flo's house in Lake Wobegon. The next year we rented the Sons of Knute temple, and after that we broke apart into separate single-family Thanksgivings.

There were simply too many of us, about 60, for that three-bedroom bungalow. There were card-tables upstairs, in the basement and in the living room. The men wedged themselves along the blue sofa and on the floor and watched football on Al's snowy TV set. Upstairs, little kids played with Lincoln logs and plastic cowboys, quietly, after Uncle Jack threatened to lock them in the garage. Sun poured in the front window, the radiators steamed, and steam drifted out from the kitchen, which was packed with aunts.

I stood by the kitchen door, next to the praying-hands plaque, talking to Aunt Marie, who wasn't allowed in the kitchen because she dropped things. My fiancée stood beside me; it was her first encounter with the family, who were trying not to look at her, and she was trying to catch my eye. She was bored to tears and needed a cigarette. "Let's go for a walk," she whispered. But it wasn't easy to escape. Poor Marie was clinging to us for dear life. She kept asking me about school, about our wedding, about anything at all—we were her life raft. She couldn't sit on the sofa, go upstairs, or enter the kitchen.

My aunts were powerful women caught up in a crusade to create vast quantities of food and stuff us with it and stuff the rest into Tupperware dishes and stuff them into the refrigerator. Marie, who married into the family, was a weak reed. She was unsure of recipes and worried about measuring accurately. My aunts stood shoulder to shoulder and whacked at things and whipped and chopped and slapped dinner together. "I have to get out of here right now," my fiancée whispered. I felt the same way, but how do you get out of your own family? "Your writing!" Marie cried. "Tell me about your writing!"

We extracted ourselves from her and put on our coats, and the moment we got out the door, I felt buoyant. We walked down the street and, free of the family, I could speak up, I could say what I thought, be vulgar, have great opinions, be original, and when I turned the corner, we could smoke a cigarette. Pall Malls. "Did you really grow up here?" my fiancée asked. I could see her point. A guy like me coming from such a dismal little town, little frame houses with dumb lawn ornaments and the people inside cooking the exact same dinners and saying the same things: Yes, I grew up here, but of course, even as a child, I had looked to distant horizons. And I regretted that my family was not more colorful. I wished we were Italians. Italians had ethnic customs. We didn't. We just had turkey for Thanksgiving. Italians had big flagons of red wine. We had pitchers of ice water. We were Sanctified Brethren.

In 1986, for my new Danish wife and stepchildren, who wanted an authentic American Thanksgiving, I fixed the traditional barbecued spareribs and the customary Thanksgiving linguini with garlic sauce on the side, and we enjoyed the old-fashioned Thanksgiving Scotch and soda. But at Thanksgiving 1965, there was no alcohol. Not a drop. My fiancée's family in Minneapolis, who were fall Methodists, were knocking down some Manhattans, I knew, and keeping them nice and fresh, and I wished we were there, instead of among the Brethren.

Thanksgiving is better when you're with somebody else's family and can enjoy their little fights. Her mother and father sparred constantly, over silly things like money, whereas my parents fought with me and fought for blood, over ultimate truths and matters of faith. That day, walking back to Al and Flo's, I knew that Vietnam was bound to come up at dinner. I could imagine my Uncle Jack saying, "Ya, well, I don't know about these protesters and this draft-card burning, but if it was up to me, I'd throw them out of college and put them to work if they don't want to go in the Army." And then I would say something about our tragic mistakes in Southeast Asia, and a few minutes later, my beloved uncle would lean forward and hiss at me and my dear aunts would purse their lips and glare and my mother would run weeping to the bathroom.

But when we got back, something else had happened, something unpleasant, everybody was very thin-lipped about it. "It's nothing," my mother said. "Don't bring it up." "What is it?" I said. "It doesn't con-

If the Indians had had an immigration policy.

cern you," she said. It concerned Uncle Jack and Aunt Dee. I gathered that he had gotten up from the football game and come to the kitchen for a drink of water and she said something and he said something back, something mean, just teasing, and she threw something at him, playfully, which happened to be a paring knife, and it made a deep scratch down his cheek.

Jack returned to the couch and resumed watching TV, bleeding profusely, shrugging off first aid. Aunt Lois ran for a washcloth, Uncle Al dabbed at him with a hanky. "It's nothing," he said. He bled all down the front of his new white shirt. Aunt Dee went down to the basement and cried and came back mad. The basement had reminded her of things in the past, of her historic struggle with Jack. "He's always saying things like that," she said. "He hasn't changed since he was nine years old." Jack would not look at her or anybody else. "I'm not mad," he said. "If the rest of you want to make a federal case out of it, go ahead. I'm just fine."

The food was portioned out to all the cardboard tables and everyone sat down in a thoughtful mood. In the kitchen, Dee and Aunt Mary were still muttering at each other: "Well, he started it." "Yes, but you could have had the decency to apologize for throwing a knife at him." "I see no point in discussing it," said Dee. "You've always taken his side and you always will." Aunt Mary lowered the boom. "You never cared a bit for this family. You didn't go visit Mother before she died and nobody was a bit surprised. You've always gone your own way. And now you're ruining this Thanksgiving." Dee fled back to the basement. We could hear her long musical sobs. Mary sat down with us in the dining room, breathing hard. Vietnam seemed like a small distant event compared to this, and if I had mentioned the war, it might've come as a great relief.

Then Uncle Al dinged his glass. "We're going to return thanks now," he said, and called up the hot air vent to diners upstairs, "Time for grace now!" He must have been awfully upset, too upset to pray, because he said, "Carl, would you return thanks," and Uncle Carl stood up and cleared his throat.

Uncle Carl was the last person you'd ask to pray, ever. For one thing, he prayed longer than anybody else in the Sanctified Brethren,

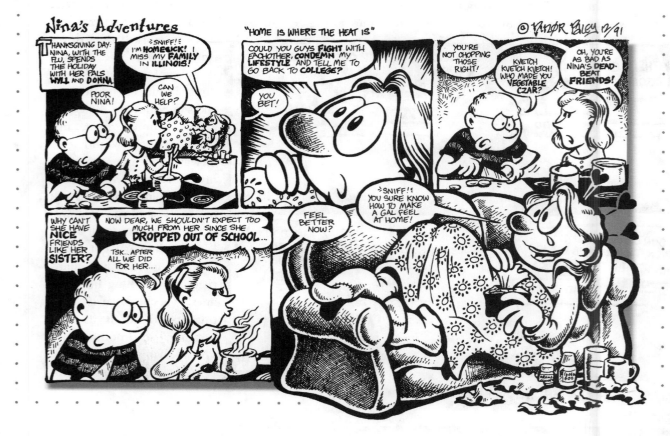

where prayers tended to cover a lot of theological ground and touch on all the main points of faith. Carl was endless. Scripture said, "Pray without ceasing," and he almost succeeded. He could pray until food got moldy. And, what was worse, when Carl came to the part of the prayer where he thanked God for sending His only begotten Son Jesus Christ to die on the cross as propitiation for our sins, he always wept.

Carl had wept in prayer for many years. Either he never got over Jesus' death, the way the rest of us had, or else it was just a bad habit he couldn't stop. He always stood and cried, helpless, his shoulders shaking. He was a sweet man with tidy gray hair, oiled, with comb tracks in it, a dapper dresser who favored bow ties – a good uncle, and it was painful to sit and listen to him cry.

He stood, and we stirred in our seats uneasily. I peeked at my fiancée, and saw she had already put a big dab of squash on her plate. She was not accustomed to table grace. I couldn't imagine she'd be ready for Uncle Carl.

Carl spoke in a clear voice toward the heating vent so the people upstairs could hear, thanking God for the food, for each other, for this day, and then for sending His only begotten son Jesus to die on Calvary's cross, and he started to sob, such a wrenching sound, his awful weeping, especially because he tried to keep talking about Jesus, and the words would hardly come out. He stopped and blew his nose and we all, one by one, started to get weepy. My fiancée wept, I cried, we all cried. I don't think we wept for Jesus so much as from exhaustion. Families can wear you out some-

times. Down in the basement, somebody was bawling. And right there, as Carl wiped his nose and everyone around the dining room table sniffled, my cousin Duke leaned forward and tossed her cookies.

Everyone had their eyes closed, and believe me, it's more vivid when you only hear it. Radio is a powerful medium. She vomited twice and gagged twice, two longs and two shorts, and staggered for the bathroom. There was some sympathetic gagging among the other children, and some men got up suddenly, even before Carl's amen, and went outdoors and leaned against the house. My aunts leaped into action and cleared the table and whipped off the tablecloth and mopped up the floor and dinner was put back in the oven while our heads settled and our appetites returned. This took about half an hour. Some people took walks, others simply stood looking out windows. Dishes were washed, the room aired out, the table reset, and eventually we came back. I felt good: Someone had vomited at the table before a meal and it was not me.

There was some question of whether to repray or not, whether the previous blessing was still in effect, and Uncle Al said a brief grace, thanking God for His mercy. We ate. Tentatively at first, but we hit our stride and finished up strong, with pumpkin pie. Duke was so mortified she began her long career of not vomiting. Twenty-five years of relative calm. Uncle Jack died a few years later, and Aunt Dee followed in 1982: May they rest in peace. Happy Thanksgiving. Life is good. Even when it is lousy, it is still good, and thank God for it.

The World According to Student Bloopers

by Richard Lederer

It is truly astounding what havoc students can wreak upon the chronicles of the human race. I have pasted together the following "history" of the world from genuine student bloopers collected by teachers throughout the United States, from eighth grade through college level.

Read carefully, and you will learn a lot:

Ancient Egypt was inhabited by mummies, and they all wrote in hydraulics. They lived in the Sarah Dessert and traveled by Camelot. The climate of the Sarah is such that the inhabitants have to live elsewhere, so certain areas of the dessert are cultivated by irritation.

The pyramids are a range of mountains between France and Spain. The Egyptians built the pyramids in the shape of a huge triangular cube.

The Bible is full of interesting caricatures. In the first book of the Bible, Guinessis, Adam and Eve were created from an apple tree. One of their children, Cain, asked, "Am I my brother's son?"

God asked Abraham to sacrifice Isaac on Mount Montezuma. Jacob, son of Isaac, stole his brother's birthmark. Jacob was a patriarch who brought up his 12 sons to be patriarchs, but they did not take to it. One of Jacob's sons, Joseph, gave refuse to the Israelites.

Pharaoh forced the Hebrew slaves to make bread without straw. Moses led them to the Red Sea, where they made unleavened bread, which is bread made without any ingredients. Afterwards, Moses went up on Mount Cyanide to get the ten commandments. He died before he ever reached Canada.

David Cohen

David was a Hebrew king skilled at playing the liar. He fought with the Finkelsteins, a race of people who lived in Biblical times. Solomon, one of David's sons, had 300 wives and 700 porcupines.

Later came Job, who had one trouble after another. Eventually, he lost all his cattle and all his children and had to go live alone with his wife in the desert.

The Greeks were a highly sculptured people, and without them we wouldn't have history. The Greeks invented three kinds of columns — corinthian, ironic, and dorc — and built the Apocalypse. They also had myths. A myth is a female moth.

One myth says that the mother of Achilles dipped him in the River Stynx until he became intolerable. Achilles appears in *The Iliad*, by Homer. Homer also wrote *The Oddity*, in which Penelope was the last hardship that Ulysses endured on his journey. Actually, Homer was not written by Homer but by another man of that name.

Socrates was a famous Greek teacher who went around giving people advice. They killed

THE LOST CONTINENT OF ATLANTIS, AND THE REASON FOR ITS DEMISE, ARE DISCOVERED.

©CHRONICLE FEATURES 1992

MAKING POPCORN—200,000,000 b.c.

CALLEN

doing. When they fought with the Persians, the Greeks were outnumbered because the Persians had more men.

Eventually, the Romans conquered the Geeks. History calls people Romans because they never stayed in one place for very long.

Julius Caesar extinguished himself on the battlefields of Gaul. The Ides of March murdered him because they thought he was going to be made king. Dying, he gasped out the words "Tee hee, Brutus." Nero was a cruel tyranny who would torture his poor subjects by playing the fiddle to them.

Rome came to have too many luxuries and baths. At Roman banquets, the guests wore garlics in their hair. They took two baths in two days, and that's the cause of the fall of Rome. Today, Rome is full of fallen arches.

Then came the Middle Ages, when everyone was middle-aged. King Alfred conquered the Dames. King Arthur lived in the Age of Shivery with brave knights on prancing horses and beautiful women. King Harold mustarded his troops before the Battle of Hastings. Joan of Arc was cannonized by Bernard Shaw. And victims of the blue-bonnet plague grew boobs on their necks. Finally, Magna Carta provided that no free man should be hanged twice for the same offense.

In midevil times most people were alliterate. The greatest writer of the futile ages was Chaucer, who wrote many poems and verses and also wrote literature. During this time, people put on morality plays about ghosts, goblins, virgins, and other mythical creatures. Another story was about William Tell, who shot an arrow through an apple while standing on his son's head.

The Renaissance was an age in which more individuals felt the value of their human being. Martin Luther was nailed to the church door at Wittenberg for selling papal indulgences. He died a horrible death, being excommunicated by a bull. It was the painter Donatello's interest in the female nude that made him the father of the Renaissance.

The government of England was a limited mockery. From the womb of Henry VIII, Protestanism was born. He found walking dif-

him. Socrates died from an overdose of wedlock. After his death, his career suffered a dramatic decline.

In the Olympic Games, Greeks ran races, jumped, hurled the biscuits, and threw the java. The reward to the victor was a coral wreath.

The government of Athens was democratic because people took the law into their own hands. There were no wars in Greece, as the mountains were so high that they couldn't climb over to see what their neighbors were ficult because he had an abbess on his knee.

Queen Elizabeth was the "Virgin Queen." As a queen she was a success. When Elizabeth exposed herself before her troops, they all shouted "hurrah." Then her navy went out and defeated the Spanish Armadillo.

It was an age of great inventions and discoveries. Gutenberg invented the Bible. Another important invention was the circulation of blood. Sir Walter Raleigh is a historical figure because he invented cigarettes and started smoking. And Sir Francis Drake circumcised the world with a 100-foot clipper.

The greatest writer of the Renaissance was William Shakespeare. Shakespeare was born in the year 1564, supposedly on his birthday. He never made much money and is famous only because of his plays. He lived at Windsor with his merry wives, writing tragedies, comedies, and errors.

In one of Shakespeare's famous plays, Hamlet rations out his situation by relieving himself in a long soliloquy. His mind is filled with the filth of incestuous sheets which he pours over every time he sees his mother. In another play, Lady Macbeth tries to convince Macbeth to kill the King by attacking his man-

hood. The proof that the witches in *Macbeth* were supernatural is that no one could eat what they cooked.

The clown in *As You Like It* is named Touchdown, and Romeo and Juliet are an example of a heroic couplet.

Writing at the same time as Shakespeare was Miguel Cervantes. He wrote *Donkey Hote*. The next great author was John Milton. Milton wrote *Paradise Lost*. Then his wife died and he wrote *Paradise Regained*.

During the Renaissance, America began. Christopher Columbus was a great navigator who discovered America while cursing about the Atlantic. His ships were called the Nina, the Pinta, and the Santa Fe.

Later, the Pilgrims crossed the ocean, and this was called Pilgrim's Progress. The winter of 1620 was a hard one for the settlers. Many people died and many babies were born. Captain John Smith was responsible for all this.

One of the causes of the Revolutionary War was the English put tacks in their tea. Also, the colonists would send their parcels through the post without stamps. During the War, the Red Coats and Paul Revere were throwing balls over stone walls. The dogs were barking and the peacocks crowing. Finally, the colonists won the War and no longer had to pay for taxis.

Delegates from the original 13 states formed the Contented Congress. Thomas Jefferson, a Virgin, and Benjamin Franklin were two singers of the Declaration of Independence. Franklin had gone to Boston carrying all his clothes in his pocket and a loaf of bread under each arm. He invented electricity by rubbing two cats backwards and declared, "A horse divided against itself cannot stand." Franklin died in 1790 and is still dead.

George Washington married Martha Curtis and in due time became the Father of Our Country. His farewell address was Mount Vernon.

Soon the Constitution of the United States was adopted to secure domestic hostility. Under the Constitution the people enjoyed the right to keep bare arms.

Abraham Lincoln became America's greatest Precedent. Lincoln's mother died in infancy, and he was born in a log cabin which he built with his own hands. When Lincoln was president, he wore only a tall silk hat. He said, "In onion there is strength."

Abraham Lincoln wrote the Gettysburg Address while traveling from Washington to Gettysburg on the back of an envelope. He also freed the slaves by signing the Emasculation Proclamation.

On the night of April 14, 1865, Lincoln went to the theater and got shot in his seat by one of the actors in a moving picture show. The believed assinator was John Wilkes Booth, a supposingly insane actor. This ruined Booth's career.

Meanwhile in Europe, the enlightenment was a reasonable time. Voltaire invented electricity and also wrote a book called *Candy*. Gravity was invented by Isaac Walton. It is chiefly noticeable in the autumn, when the apples are falling off the trees.

Johann Bach wrote a great many musical compositions and had a large number of children. In between, he practiced on an old spinster which he kept up in his attic. Bach died from 1750 to the present.

Bach was the most famous composer in the world, and so was Handel. Handel was half German, half Italian, and half English. He was very large.

Beethoven wrote music even though he was deaf. He was so deaf he wrote loud music. He took long walks in the forest even when everyone was calling for him. Beethoven expired in 1827 and later died for this.

France was in a very serious state. The French Revolution was accomplished before it happened and catapulted into Napoleon. During the Napoleonic Wars, the crowned heads of Europe were trembling in their shoes. Then the Spanish gorillas came down from the hills and nipped at Napoleon's flanks. Napoleon became ill with bladder problems and was very tense and unrestrained. He wanted an heir to inherit his power, but since Josephine was a baroness, she couldn't have any children.

The sun never set on the British Empire because the British Empire is in the East and the sun sets in the West. Queen Victoria was the longest queen. She sat on a thorn for 63 years. She was a moral woman who practiced virtue. Her reclining years and finally the end of her life were exemplatory of a great personality. Her death was the final event which ended her reign.

The nineteenth century was a time of a great many thoughts and inventions. People stopped reproducing by hand and started reproducing by machine. The invention of the steamboat caused a network of rivers to spring up. Cyrus McCormick invented the McCormick raper, which did the work of a hundred men. Samuel Morse invented a code of telepathy. Louis Pasteur discovered a cure for rabbis. Charles Darwin was a naturalist who wrote the *Organ of the Species*. Madman Curie discovered radio. And Karl Marx became one of the Marx brothers.

The First World War, caused by the assignation of the Arch-Duck by an anahist, ushered in a new error in the anals of human history.

SERFS UP

My Obituary

by Raymond Lesser

I looked at two different obituary pages yesterday. The one from the *New York Times* had headlines like: **Dr. Arnold Osterman, 85, Olympic Gold Medalist and Inventor of Heart Bypass Surgery**. And: **Helen Wall, Broadway Star, Philanthropist, and Mother of Senator**. On the other hand in the *Cleveland Plain Dealer*, my hometown daily, the obituaries, which featured much bigger headlines, read like this: **Emma Kowalski, 88, Made Marvelous Coffee Cakes**. And: **Henry Timmons, Was Gardener, Brewed Beer**.

It made me think about what my own obituary might say. (**Raymond Lesser, Liked to Drink Coffee and Read Newspapers**.) It dawned on me that I probably hadn't done anything that would rate an obituary in the *New York Times*, even if I died in New York. (**Raymond S. Lesser, Loyal Out-of-Town Subscriber, Is Found Dead in Adult Theatre Near Times Square**.)

This doesn't really concern me at the moment since I intend to live for many more years and do many great and memorable things. But seeing as how I'm already 37 and haven't yet done anything that great or well-known, at least not anything the *New York Times* has noticed, I began to wonder what it would be that would make my obituary special.

I don't want to be remembered because of my relationship with someone else who is well-known. (**Husband of Woman Who Claims to Have Been Repeatedly Visited by Aliens Dies of Mysterious Causes**.) Nor do I want to be recalled as a subject of cutting edge medicine. (**Courageous Recipient of First Transplanted Sheep Heart, Goose Liver, and Beef Tongue Is Run Over by**

We are gathered here today to honor the memory of Frederick P. Zoltin, who lived to the age of 89 years and never had a clue.

Bus; Memorial Service to Be Held at Jack's Deli.) And I obviously don't want to be known because of something bad I did. (**Raymond Lesser, Fisherman, Caught Last Remaining Blue-Striped Bass and Pan-Fried It for Supper**.)

I would like to be known for some great achievement in sports, but I think that is unlikely. (**Rabid Ray Lesser, Became Pro-Hockey Star After Learning to Skate at Age of 38**.) Nor do I stand much chance of making a great scientific discovery. (**R.S. Lesser, Discovered Gateway to Alpha-Centauri While Searching for His Car Keys**.)

But I still have a great deal of confidence that I will eventually do something memorable. (**R. Lesser, 88, Always Had a Great Deal of Confidence**.) Maybe I'll organize a successful consumer protest group. (**Well Known Activist Passes; Began Boycott Against Tags in Men's Underwear**.) Perhaps I'll come up with an unforgettable fad. (**Creator of Edible Telephones Dies at His Palm Beach Estate**.) Or I might write a great exposé. (**Reporter Who Discovered Link Between the Mafia and All Lousy**

Home-Delivered Pizza Is Found Dead in a Crate of Anchovies.)

Of course it's impossible to predict the circumstances of one's own demise and to get nostalgic about it is beyond morbid, it's an egotistic perversion. (**Raymond Lesser, Writer and Egotistical Pervert, Chokes on His Own Words.**) However, it is a wonderful way to focus on what it is in life that one desires to do but has not yet been accomplished, or perhaps even attempted. (**Outdoorsman, 93, Failed in Sixteen Attempts to Climb Mt. Everest.**)

It certainly is difficult to motivate oneself to attempt something meaningful after a busy day, or busy week of doing everything that has to get done. But the alternatives aren't very pleasant to think about. (**Man, 62, Is Found Dead in Front of His TV. Neighbors Can't Remember His Name but Knew He Liked to Watch Baseball.**)

It's easier if you start with small changes. (**Rebel TV Viewer, 62, Threw Out His Remote Control and Got Up to Change His Own Channels.**) Soon you'll be doing something worth talking about. (**Near-sighted Neighbor Is Mourned; Well Remembered for Umpiring Playground Softball Games.**) And ultimately, who knows what the possibilities are. (**Ray "Johnny Mapleseed" Lesser, Who Planted a Million Shade Trees, to Be Buried in His Orchard, Now a National Park.**) That's right, if you try hard enough, anything is possible! (**Outdoorsman, 93, Who Failed in Sixteen Attempts to Climb Mt. Everest Has His Ashes Sprinkled on the Summit.**)

Zen and the Art Of Lotto

by Oscar London

PIPEDREAM

Why do you lose at Lotto while some visitor from Mazatlán wins $24,000,000, using the first six numbers on his Green Card? Why do you lose at Lotto when your mother always told you that you were born to win? Why do you lose at Lotto when you've promised God that if you could win but $3,000,000, you'd be eternally grateful?

The reason you lose at Lotto, of course, is impure thinking. At my ashram in Berkeley, I, Baba Reesh Dom Luk, teach Lotto players how to banish impure thinking. For a voluntary contribution of $5.00, you too can learn to approach a Lotto machine with pure thinking.

Do you suppose you can drive up to just any 7-Eleven, saunter over to a Lotto machine and ask the clerk for ten dollars' worth of Quick Pick – and expect to win? Well, often as not, my friends, you will lose. You will lose because your thoughts are impure.

Did you contemplate the prithma of the 7-Eleven as you entered? In other words, had the franchise realized its essential Seven-

"I WANT YOU TO TAKE TWO OF THESE CAPSULES WHENEVER YOU FEEL LUCKY."

Elevishment or had it merely achieved midthra (Three-Fivishment) and hoped you wouldn't know the difference? Ah, you didn't notice? Your mind, instead, was consumed with an impure thought – consumed, that is to say, with komonbabi, or gambling lust.

The clerk adversely reacts to your komonbabi as he summons your Quick Pick numbers on the Lotto machine. The Lotto machine, resonating to his negatively charged fingertips, spews out six impure – or losing – numbers.

If you attend my ashram, you will learn that the first two numbers of any winning combination of six reside within your thighs, the middle two numbers separately occupy your hips, and the last two numbers live in your neck. You will learn these winning numbers through meditation, pinching and chanting. Some weeks may pass before your impure thoughts sufficiently lift to allow the winning numbers within your body to become manifest.

Then you will walk humbly into a 7-Eleven and feel a tingle, say, in one thigh, one hip, and the left side of your neck. Certain of winning $5, you will ask the clerk in a supremely

The Lottery Commission Bowling Team

indifferent tone of voice, "Ten dollars Quick Pick, please." When the numbers are announced that evening, you will have won $5 unless, of course, some of the tingling you experienced was due to sciatica.

After nine weeks at my ashram, you will approach the Lotto machine, tingling in all six centers. When you ask for ten dollars' worth of Quick Pick, the serene clerk will instruct the Lotto machine to spew out 60 random numbers arranged in ten rows of six numbers each. You will go home, undress and bathe. You will don your silk robe with the Lotto 6/49 logo on the back. You will sit down on the couch before the TV set and assume the Lotto's position – legs bent under you, right hand outstretched with palm up. You will empty your head of impure thoughts.

When the winning numbers are flashed on the screen, you will announce to your family and friends that you have a midrin, or headache, and must step outside for a little while.

You will walk to the nearest mailbox and post your winning ticket in an envelope addressed to me, Reesh Dom Luk, P.O. Box 7123, Berkeley, CA, 94707. Why must you send me your winning ticket? Because the impurest thought of all is holenchilada – or greed – and the purest thought of all is sparchanji – charity.

You might well ask if your winning ticket will be used to enlarge my vroom vroom or, as the IRS has termed it, my fleet of Rolls Royces. I can only point out that the path to Enlightenment is an arduous one, calling for a fully independent suspension, rack and pinion steering, a wet bar and disk brakes.

Or would you rather that I, Baba Reesh Dom Luk, drive a Buick?

Callahan

Distributed by Levin Represents

"I'm going to have to go with prize number 3, Bob."

Memories

by Bob Maier

I've heard losing your memory is a sign of old age. I just can't remember where I heard it.

I was trying hard not to remember the correlation between forgetfulness and senescence Thursday morning when I told the security guard at the office building I had forgotten my ID badge. I explained that I normally stop just past the security checkpoint and put my badge in my briefcase, but on Wednesday I had been in a hurry and left the badge in the pocket of my gray suit.

The guard, who is about the same age as my younger brother's second daughter, listened patiently with the polite look well brought-up young people reserve for tiresome old fossils. When I came to the part about making a mental note to move the badge from my coat pocket to the table where I keep my wallet and change, and remembering it perfectly, but not until I was coming through the office door that morning, instead of chuckling along with me she made the kind of soothing "there, there, it's all right" noises people use to comfort small, helpless children. She gave me a temporary pass and urged me to "have a nice day."

When I walked up to the security desk the next morning, it wasn't déjà vu; I knew I had been there before and for the very same rea-

son. My ID badge was still in the pocket of a suit I was not wearing. The security guard politely failed to mention how recently we had done all this, but I caught her looking in my mouth to see if I still had any real teeth.

Pressing my thumb and forefinger together as a reminder, I walked directly to my desk and called my home phone. After my answering machine picked up, I left a message reminding myself to put my ID badge in my briefcase, and to put the suit that needed alterations and the coat that needed cleaning by the door so I wouldn't forget them again. While I was at it, I reminded myself to call my brother and my parents (I had been meaning to do so for the last two months) and to check the car's odometer to see how overdue it was for an oil change. As I finished the message I forgot who I was talking to, dropped into my standard voice mail closing and told myself I'd talk to me later.

About an hour after that I saw one of my

SOME PEOPLE MAY SUFFER MEMORY LOSS AS THEY AGE BECAUSE THEY'VE SHIFTED THE JOB OF REMEMBERING FROM AREAS BEHIND THE FOREHEAD TO A LESS EFFICIENT PART OF THE BRAIN.

AND SOME OF US...

DON'T KNOW WHERE THE HECK IT IS.

the NO-BRAINER CAPER.

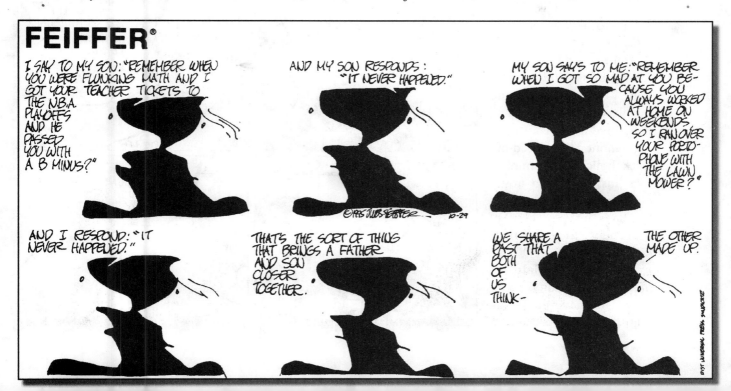

colleagues by the coffee machine. "I paged you half an hour ago. Why haven't you called me?" he asked.

Instinctively I patted my left side. No beeper. I had forgotten to pick it up from the night stand.

I went home for lunch that day. I put the ID badge in my briefcase and put the beeper on my belt. I put the suit that needed alterations and the coat that needed cleaning in the car. I left a note on the refrigerator telling me to call my brother and to take the car in for an oil change. I still had a few minutes before I had to start back to the office, so I called my mother.

I told her about how much trouble I was having remembering things and that I thought it was because I was getting old. She chuckled. "Don't you remember what you told me years ago when I thought I was losing my memory?"

Sheepishly, I admitted I did not.

"You're not forgetting things because you're getting old. You've always had a bad memory. You just don't remember that either."

Need Time? Need a Life? Get a Husband and a Wife

by Colin McEnroe

OK, here's a column, but I have to be honest: My heart is not in this.

I have been away for six weeks, ostensibly to start work on a new book, but more truthfully to get to know my one-year-old son and heir, Joseph F. McEnroe, better than I got to know him through the rattle and buzz of commutin' and workin'.

I found out what goes on in my house while I am away all day: Real life.

It turns out I like diapering and bottle-feeding and cooking and dog-tending and lying on a blanket with my little boy, gazing up at the intersections of sky and tree. So does my wife. In fact, we like doing all that stuff together, and neither of us is all that crazy about having a job.

So here is what I figure:

We need a husband.

So do a lot of people, but the good news is: We're willing to settle for a defective husband.

You know all those best-selling books intended to help women understand that they have been hurling their love at unreciprocating, emotionally closed-off, workaholic, uncommunicative husbands who aren't even any good in bed?

That's just the kind of husband we are in the market for.

It could turn into an important national program. You have to assume that, if even 10 percent of the women who bought these books saw the light and dumped their defective husbands, there would be quite a few of them wandering the American social tundra, watching big-screen television in sports bars, going for long rides on weekends, whatever.

We are prepared to offer one of those men a marriage — a marriage in which all of those qualities his first wife considered to be major liabilities would be transformed into whopping assets.

Think about it, men. Did your first wife say these things about you?

• "You never talk about your feelings." This is fine with us. We understand that it is hard for some men to talk about their feelings, and, anyway, we don't want to know anything about yours. I have feelings; my wife has feelings; the baby has feelings; the dogs have feel-

ings. That's plenty of feelings. Keep yours bottled up. They're really none of our business.

• "You'd rather be out at a sports event with your male friends than at home." No problem. You and the boys can go to as many games as you want. Rent a *pied a terre* next to Fenway Park for all we care. We mainly need your paycheck and health insurance.

• "You're not tender in bed." Needless to say, whether or not you are tender in bed is strictly between you and the dogs, which is who you'll be sleeping with.

• "You work late all the time." We want you to work late. It keeps you out of our hair, plus we need the overtime for our many expenses. So by all means, work late. For that matter, cheat on us. We mean it.

You may be wondering: What would the new husband get out of this arrangement?

Well, as your spouse, my wife and I would pick up your dry cleaning.

Plus, there's the tax break you'd get from all these new dependents.

Also, we are the kind of family you can be proud of. You could keep our picture on your desk. You could tell visitors to your office, "Yep, this is my wife, this is my husband, and this is their son Joey."

The most important thing we have to give you, however, is something you've never had before in your life: a relationship that makes absolutely no emotional or psychic demands on you.

You, the withdrawn guy, have had problems in the past with women who loved too much. We promise not to love you at all. If any of us starts to feel even a glimmer of love for you, we'll go for counseling. You probably won't want to come because that would involve talking about your feelings. Plus, Bears-Dolphins is on "Monday evening. Fine. We'll go without you. We'll write up an executive summary for you to read.

If our arrangement is successful, I'd probably write a best-seller on the new Non-Intimate Co-Nuptialist movement. Then we'd have to go on "Donahue" to promote it.

What do you mean you wouldn't do that? After everything I've done for you, you wouldn't go on a lousy talk show for me?

What do you mean I'm making demands? I'm your spouse, for gosh sakes! Is it too much ask that you turn off t game while I'm talking you? Now, listen...

AMERICAN MALE CLUB'S *eight* RECOGNIZED BREEDS OF MEN

TORMENTED ARTIST
LIFE IS MEANINGLESS. JOY IS AN ILLUSION. WE HAVE BUT DEATH TO LOOK FORWARD TO.

BRILLIANT SOCIOPATH
SNIF?
HIM

SELF-HATING OVERACHIEVER
HOW CAN YOU REALLY LOVE ME IF I ONLY HAVE SEVEN PULITZERS? I'M WORTHLESS!

DUMB REPUBLICAN
DON'T LIKE HOMELESSNESS? TOXIC DUMPING? THEN GET OUT OF AMERICA, YOU HOMO COMMIE!

SMART REPUBLICAN
YOU HAVE NAIVE, MISGUIDED VIEWS. SOCIAL JUSTICE IS IMPOSSIBLE. FACE IT. SELL OUT.

GORGEOUS AIRHEAD

TRUSTWORTHY BORE
I'LL BE THERE AT EXACTLY 6:03 AND THEN I'LL SHOW YOU MY NEW BOOK ON ACCOUNTING, OK?

BOLTER
HONEY, LET'S DISCUSS COMMIT...
FOOSH

©1990 JENNIFER BERMAN

How to Give Up Self-Improvement

by Susan Moon

I want to talk to you today about the importance of giving up self-improvement. This is one of our hardest tasks, as we train ourselves to follow the Buddha Way. In this modern age, we are met at every turn by new and tempting opportunities to improve ourselves. We are offered everything from workshops on how to be a better parent to classes in strengthening the quadriceps. We are so deeply habituated to this way of thinking that we do not even recognize it in ourselves. This is the great danger. How many of you first began to sit zazen with the hope that it would in some way make you a better person? For many of us it may take years of hard practice before we are completely sure that we have hoped in vain. Buddhism teaches us that everything always changes, but we must finally admit that it does not change for the better.

When old Bush Wak was still master at the monastery on Lazy Man Mountain, a young monk with flabby thighs said to him, "My mind dwells always on the five desires (food, sex, sleep, fame, wealth). Last night I ate all the lychee nuts in the monastery storeroom. How can I conquer my weakness and become a better person?"

"You ricebag, you!" snarled Bush Wak. "Who wants to be a good person? Lie down without delay and take a nap till the feeling passes. How can you be awakened if you are not asleep?"

Za Phu has given us this verse:
The old ricebag and the young ricebag grumble
  on Lazy Man Mountain.
How they annoy each other with their unpleas-
  ant personalities!
The young ricebag falls asleep.
When he awakes he will still be a sickly ricebag.

"But what's so bad about self-improvement?" you may ask. Perhaps you have disagreeable character traits or week knees that interfere with your functioning in everyday life. You may be eager to give up an addiction to cocaine or a habit of constantly interrupting the conversation of other people. But the very first habit you must give up is the habit of self-improvement. You can worry about the other things later. There may be a time and place in your life for self-improvement, but the zendo is not the place, and now is not the time. Put it off.

Giving up self-improvement is easier said than done. Each of us must walk this path alone, going nowhere. But as your teacher, I can suggest to you some skillful means by which you may at least break the habit of mending your ways, and I can offer you some guidelines by which you may measure your progress on this pathless path.

I would like to ask that you take two weeks of your life to devote yourself to relinquishing self-betterment. If you conscientiously follow the eightfold path that I here describe, I am confident you will be pleased with the lack of results.

1. As soon as you get up in the morning, stand before the mirror, look your reflection in the eye, and ask yourself ten times, "Who wants to be a better person anyway?"

2. Before going to sleep each night, tell yourself ten times, "Every day in every way I am getting less attached to self-improvement."

3. For these two weeks, withdraw from all therapy programs, yoga classes, harpsichord lessons, courses in wilderness survival, or other educational pursuits. There will be time to pick up where you left off, when you are free from the need to achieve.

4. For the duration of the program, do not follow any special diets. Make a half-hearted attempt to eat whatever is lying around the house forgotten. This is the time to use up the jar of cocktail onions, the stale crackers, the rest of those little silver balls for decorating cakes, and other such things you may find in the back of the cupboard.

5. Walk slowly in place for twenty minutes a day, while repeating monotonously, "There is no attainment, with nothing to attain." It takes a full twenty minutes for your body to register the fact that it is not benefiting either from an increased heart rate or the secretion of stress-reducing epinephrines into the bloodstream. This is an advanced practice, demanding constant mindfulness so that you don't go anywhere or get any exercise. At first you may need to check your pulse periodically to be sure that it stays the same.

6. Keep a chart on which you daily mark as high or low your level of attachment in the following areas:
• mentally healthy interpersonal interactions
• physical well-being
• productive work
• spiritual enlightenment

Remember, you are looking for low attachment, not high achievement.

7. From the daily TV program guide, select the program that interests you the least. Be honest with yourself. Then watch this program with a glazed expression. More advanced students should tape the program on a VCR and watch it a second time.

8. Sit on a round black cushion and face the wall. Don't think about anything. Breathe.

If you follow these instructions with meticulous effort, you will find at the end of two weeks that you have not only failed to improve, but you have given up the very idea of self-improvement, perceiving it at last for the hopeless task it really is.

I respectfully ask you not to waste your time. You may delude yourself by promising to give up self-improvement soon, after you have stopped biting your fingernails, lost ten pounds, or learned to jitterbug. This is a trap. Tomorrow it may be too late – in the final stages of the disease, the sufferer loses all control and those around him find themselves hiding course catalogues and health-club brochures. Bush Wak told the young monk to take a nap immediately. Remember, you are perfect already, exactly as you are. In a manner of speaking. And if you were really perfect, you wouldn't have a friend in the world.

Coupons for Sex

by Kent Nelson Moreno

The story you are about to read is true. The names have been changed to protect the guilty.

In 1988 I worked at a short-term residential facility for individuals with mental retardation. One afternoon while I was meeting with my supervisor a knock came at the door and a new employee, Cathy, came in. Cathy seemed excited about something and proceeded to tell us that she had placed her husband on a coupon program for sex. Cathy explained that her husband got thirteen coupons a month and she got two rain checks. Every time that Cathy's husband argued with her or didn't wipe his feet before he came in the house, he would lose a coupon. If Cathy's husband went the whole month without arguing with her and he wiped his feet before he came in the house, then he got an extra coupon. Cathy went on to say that she acted very aroused in the beginning of the month so her husband would use up all of his coupons early in the month, thus she would not have to worry about sex for the rest of the month.

Sadly, Cathy's husband went along with this program. Shortly after the implementation of Cathy's program, her husband began abusing prescription medications and Cathy had him committed to the state hospital. While Cathy's husband was in the state hospital, she sent him a letter saying that she wanted his wedding ring back and until she had it he would never see his clothes or stereo again. Cathy also took her husband's motorcycle and traded it in on a new motorcycle for herself.

During this same time, Cathy fell back in love with her ex–second husband and made the decision to divorce her current husband and remarry the ex–second husband.

Cathy's current husband, who was in the state hospital, found out about Cathy's rela-

117

tionship with her ex–second husband. He also learned that as long as he was in the state hospital, Cathy could not divorce him. Therefore, after the initial involuntary commitment period was up, Cathy's husband began voluntarily recommitting himself every thirty days to prevent Cathy from divorcing him.

Eventually, Cathy's husband did come out of the institution. Cathy divorced him and married her ex–second husband for the second time. Cathy's second marriage to her ex–second husband lasted less than a year. During the brief time the second marriage lasted, Cathy had her tubes untied so they could have a baby. According to Cathy, the reason the marriage did not last the first time was that they produced no offspring. When a child was not forthcoming, they learned that the ex–second husband had a low sperm count and so they decided to try artificial insemination. During this same time, Cathy had the ex–second husband arrested and thrown in jail for hitting her. After the ex–second husband got out of jail, they reunited and resumed trying for a child. Cathy and the ex–second husband parted for good in 1990...childless.

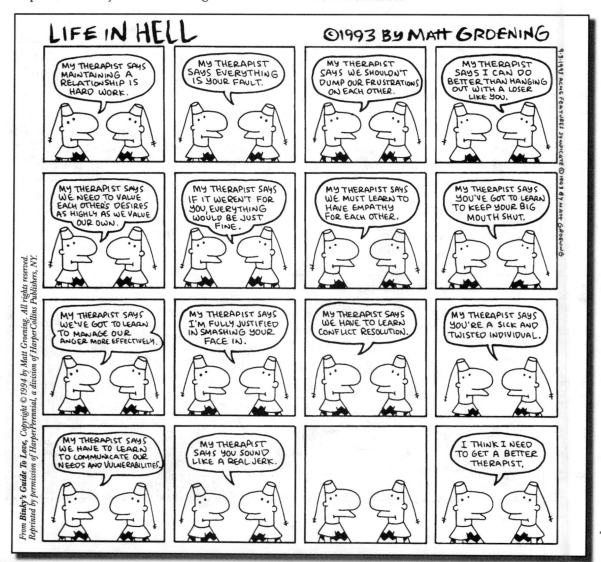

My Life as a Man
One Woman's Adventures with Testosterone

by Holly Nadler

I thought I already knew about testosterone. Men have it, right? It makes them feisty and buoyant and unfeeling and tough and resilient. Until I read a magazine article about it, I never realized that women generated even a drop of this elixir. We do, though – about 15 to 100 nanograms per deciliter of blood, as opposed to men's 300 to 1,200.

Male hormones, said my magazine, are being prescribed to women to increase the female libido. Well, fine, I thought, whip me up a milkshake of the stuff!

But then I started thinking: Perhaps testosterone could do more for me than give my sex life a lift. Did any woman really need quite so many Laura Ashleys in her closet? Or to have three friends (independent of each other) offer her a subscription to *Victoria* magazine because, they all said, "It's so you!" Could it be I contained no boy juice whatsoever?

Maybe, I thought, this was why my career as a screenwriter had suffered – because I cared too much about unreturned messages, and critiques of my work without a *soupçon* of praise.

A total overhaul in personality seemed only a prescription away. I made an appointment

with my gynecologist, and, since I had no history of heart disease (a potential side effect of cholesterol-friendly testosterone), I soon waltzed into the drugstore with a prescription for methyltestosterone, 5 milligrams daily. I was, as they say in steroid-popping, muscle-building circles, on the bus.

Nothing happened.

For several weeks, I carefully snipped the 10-milligram tabs in half, gazing wistfully at the grains that fell away into the sink. And then I *really* got on the bus. Whereas athletes might boost their daily intake into the hundreds of milligrams, I modestly swallowed an entire 10-milligram pill.

Have you ever seen the sequel to the *He-Man and the Masters of the Universe* cartoon,

when He-Man's timid twin sister dons battle gear and, raising her glinting sword, cries "I am She-ra!"

That will give you an idea of how I felt after a few days of cranking up my milligrams: Fierce. Centered. Grounded to some elemental terrestrial-cum-galactic source of power.

First, I cut my hair. For 20 years I'd worn it long and tousled, like the mane of a Daphne du Maurier heroine. In recent months, since we'd moved to New England, I had apprenticed myself to the real estate trade, conducted historical walking tours, and pounded the beat for a local newspaper. I decided I wanted to be taken seriously, taken for someone upwardly mobile. My haircutter lopped off a good eight or ten inches of dead tresses.

Next I discovered a new ease in placing business calls. I found out how normal professional people operate: You phone, you steel yourself against the obscure antagonism of someone's secretary, you leave your name or break through to the boss. You yak, find out what you need to know, crack a joke, laugh heartily at his or her joke, hang up, and go fold a load of laundry. What's the big frigging deal?

But as some of my quality of life issues moved into the plus column, I became aware that others had slid into the minus column.

It was about my walking tours. Since going on testosterone, I'd endured only tepid audiences, wondering why, day after day, I faced what stand-up comics call a tough room. They

"No KIDDING? YOU'RE REALLY A MAN? WHAT A COINCIDENCE! I'M REALLY A WOMAN!"

still chuckled in all the predictable spots, but seldom did I detect what only the summer before I'd seen on virtually all of their faces — a look of pleased absorption. I had, it seemed, lost my ability to delight.

And my voice had changed. Each morning, I would record a new tour message on the answering machine. While I spoke, I felt as friendly and engaging as ever, and I carefully and consciously spun energy and interest into my little spiel. Yet listening to the tape afterward, I was shocked to hear how flat I sounded.

I was shaken with insight. This explained everything about the battle of the sexes! About all those husbands dragged into counseling, sitting shattered and confused as they murmured mournfully, "But I do care for her. Can't she sense it?"

Having lost my ability to charm, I wanted it back again. Even if it meant an ebb in my tough professional edge or my sex drive, or sweating bullets over phone calls, or yawning over football talk. I quit the methyltestosterone.

Two days after going cold turkey, I escorted a small band of tourists on a walking tour past a row of whaling captains' houses and I discovered my knack was back. I had them.

I, who have straddled both genders, am a dazed woman. It's strange, kicking a drug. You wonder why you needed so desperately to get away from yourself when it feels so damn good to come home.

A recent survey found that a large percentage of men are afraid to admit to incompetence.

They manage to LOOK capable whether they know what they're doing or not.

That's not so bad if they're mowing a lawn...

but what if they're running the country?

Odds & Ends

THE THIN LINE BETWEEN SQUARE + COOL.

IDIOT.

IDIOT.

©1993 BY PS MUELLER.

Ah... how it doth renew one's soul to behold again the first signs of spring in the city...

©1996 PETER D. HANNAN

Story Minute ©1994 CAROL LAY
"GUARDIAN ANGEL"

THE CABBIE HAD NEVER HELPED DELIVER A BABY BEFORE...

...AND IT IMMEDIATELY GAVE HIM A SENSE OF RESPONSIBILITY FOR HER YOUNG LIFE.

THE MOTHER, A SNOB, TRIED TO GET RID OF HIM BY GIVING HIM A THOUSAND DOLLAR TIP...

...BUT THE CABBIE PUT IT INTO A SAVINGS ACCOUNT HE STARTED FOR THE LITTLE GIRL.

THE MOTHER DIDN'T WANT HIM TO ASSOCIATE WITH THEM IN ANY WAY...

...BUT HE MANAGED TO KEEP A WATCHFUL EYE ON THE LITTLE GIRL BETWEEN SHIFTS.

HE MADE SURE SHE WAS NEVER CAUGHT IN THE RAIN...

...AND, LATER, HE DISCOURAGED DISREPUTABLE LADS FROM TRYING TO MAKE TIME WITH HER.

ONE DAY HE FOUND A SUITABLE MATE FOR HER SO HE MADE SURE THEY SHARED A RIDE TOGETHER.

WHEN SHE FINALLY MARRIED THE MAN, HE FELT HIS RESPONSIBILITY FOR HER WAS ENDED.

BUT A YEAR LATER HE FOUND HER BACK IN THE CAB GIVING BIRTH TO TWINS.

AT THIS RATE, HE'D NEVER BE ABLE TO RETIRE.

Betting with God

by Steve Olstad

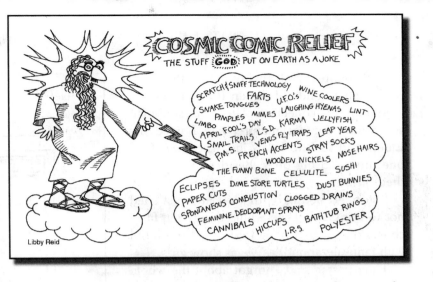

COSMIC COMIC RELIEF
THE STUFF GOD PUT ON EARTH AS A JOKE

SCRATCH & SNIFF TECHNOLOGY   WINE COOLERS
SNAKE TONGUES   FARTS   U.F.O.'s
PIMPLES   MIMES   LAUGHING HYENAS   LINT
LIMBO   FOOL'S DAY
APRIL   SNAIL TRAILS   L.S.D.   KARMA   JELLYFISH
P.M.S.   VENUS FLY TRAPS   LEAP YEAR
FRENCH ACCENTS   STRAY SOCKS
WOODEN NICKELS   NOSE HAIRS
THE FUNNY BONE   CELLULITE   SUSHI
ECLIPSES   DIME STORE TURTLES   DUST BUNNIES
PAPER CUTS
SPONTANEOUS COMBUSTION   CLOGGED DRAINS
FEMININE DEODORANT SPRAYS
CANNIBALS   HICCUPS   BATHTUB RINGS
I.R.S.   POLYESTER

Libby Reid

Things can get a little boring on the farm so I sort of got into this thing of making little bets with God, just something to pass the time. To make it interesting, there'd be money riding on the bets! I started out small with silly little bets like, "OK, God, I'll bet You two dollars that I don't get a flat tire before I get to the driveway." I'd get there without a flat, so I'd win two bucks.

Or say I'd be on my way into town, and I'd bet, "OK, if Fred's truck is parked at McDonald's, I win a buck. If it's not there, You do." I'd drive past McDonald's and suppose Fred's truck wasn't there... He'd win a buck. Did I mention that Fred hung out at McDonald's most of the time? There were lots of little bets like that.

As time went on, I made the bets more challenging and some got downright hair-raising. For instance, "Hey, if it rains before I get back to the barn, You win." Note that I was driving a slow old tractor and sometimes, I'd even make this bet when there were clouds in the sky!

The way we'd settle up accounts went like this: each Sunday when I went to church, I'd already figured out who was up for the week. Say He was up a few bucks. Well, when the collection plate came around, I'd drop in what I owed. Now, say I was up a buck or two or whatever. In that case, when the plate came around, I'd just take my winnings out before passing it on. Some weeks were just great and I'd pocket twenty, maybe thirty dollars or more! If that was the case, I'd be sure and sit in the back of the church so when the plate came my way, it would be good and full.

Then I got dumb and I suppose a little greedy. One day as I was driving into town on my way to the McDonald's, I made a bet. "OK, I bet You ONE THOUSAND DOLLARS that Fred's truck will be in the parking lot of McDonald's by the time I get there." (This really wasn't fair, in a way. Fred had called me and told me to meet him there for lunch.)

Guess what? When I got to McDonald's, Fred's truck wasn't there! Talk about spine tingles! Whoa! Later, Fred said that his engine had vapor lock and had broken down about a block away. Coincidence? I don't think so.

THE FILING CABINET OF THE GODS

LIFE

DEATH

MISC.

MUELLER

WELL OF COURSE I ANSWER MY OWN PHONE. WHEN YOU'RE OMNISCIENT, WHAT USE DO YOU HAVE FOR A SECRETARY?

PIRARO · ©1991 CHRONICLE FEATURES. 10/14   BIZARRO

So I found myself owing God a thousand bucks. That Sunday I put an IOU for the full amount in the collection plate. I just scribbled some lines for a signature, like I need the Elders and such to know just who owes God one thousand big ones. Besides, it's none of their business.

I stopped betting with God and just tried not to think about the whole thing. Yet, farm chores do get boring so I occupied my mind with fantasies about Las Vegas show girls.

Time passed and I forgot about the whole thing. I tried not to even think about it. Of course, I didn't want to pay the thousand dollars, yet on the other hand, I didn't need God mad at me right then, especially since Fred and I were going on that junket to Las Vegas the next week. I also figured I'd need the thousand bucks when I hit the slots.

Then one day, while I was working the corn, the clear sky suddenly clouded over and I heard a great rumble. Then, a flash, lightning struck the tractor I was riding on. It was like being inside a fluorescent tube that just blew up! Thank YOU-KNOW-WHO that the rubber wheels grounded me enough so I didn't fry like a bratwurst. I lived, even though it singed off all my hair and my eyebrows and I couldn't really use my bladder properly for a week or so...so much for Vegas and the show girls.

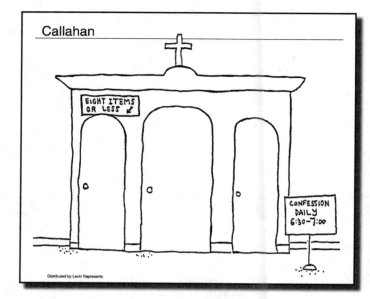

But now get this. That tractor was stopped dead in its tracks. The electrical system was shot. Like to take a guess at what it cost to repair it? That's right...one thousand dollars. Sort of makes you just sit and quiver, doesn't it?

This incident did help me put things into perspective. I guess I was sort of trying to 'fix' the bets, maybe a little, you know, betting that the sun would come up and that kind of stuff.

I've learned my lesson and wish to pass this message on to the younger generation: Don't bet with God. You may win a few and you may lose a few but payback is a bear and a half.

Yet still I have these questions. For instance, does the bill for repairing the tractor cancel the IOU or do I still owe Him a thousand bucks? And, if I do, would He be willing to go double or nothing?

Second Thoughts About the 60s

by P. J. O'Rourke

WHAT I BELIEVED IN THE 60s

Everything. You name it and I believed it. I believed love was all you needed. I believed you should be here now. I believed drugs could make everyone a better person. I believed I could hitchhike to California with thirty-five cents and people would be glad to feed me. I believed Mao was cute. I believed private property was wrong. I believed my girlfriend was a witch. I believed my parents were Nazi space monsters. I believed the university was putting saltpeter in the cafeteria food. I believed stones had souls. I believed the NLF were the good guys in Vietnam. I believed Lyndon Johnson was plotting to murder all the Negroes. I believed Yoko Ono was an artist. I believed Bob Dylan was a musician. I believed I would live forever or until twenty-one, whichever came first. I believed the world was about to end. I believed the Age of Aquarius was about to happen. I believed the I Ching said to cut classes and take over the dean's office. I believed wearing my hair long would end poverty and injustice. I believed there was a great throbbing web of psychic mucus and we were all part of it somehow. I managed to believe Gandhi and H. Rap Brown at the same time. With the exception of anything my mom and dad said, I believed everything.

WHAT CAUSED ME TO HAVE SECOND THOUGHTS

One distinct incident sent me scuttling back to Brooks Brothers. From 1969 to 1971, I was a member of a "collective" running an "underground" newspaper in Baltimore. The newspaper was called, of all things, *Harry*. When *Harry* was founded, nobody could think what to name the thing so some girl's two-year-old

THE BEAUTY OF FREE SPEECH.

REMAIN CALM.

BURN EVERYTHING!

©1992 BY P.S.MUELLER

son was asked. His grandfather was Harry and he was calling everything Harry just then, so he said, "Harry," and *Harry* was what the paper was called. It was the spirit of the age.

Harry was filled with the usual hippie blather, yea drugs and revolution, boo war and corporate profits. But it was an easy-going publication and not without a sense of humor. The want-ads section was headlined "Free Harry Classifieds Help Hep Cats and Kittens Fight Dippy Capitalist Exploitation." And once, when the office was raided by the cops (they were looking for marijuana, I might add, not sedition), *Harry* published a page-one photo of the mess left by the police search. The caption read, "*Harry* office after bust by pigs." Next to it was an identical photo captioned, "*Harry* office before bust by pigs."

Our "collective" was more interested in listening to Captain Beefheart records and testing that new invention, the water bed, than in overthrowing the state. And some of the more radical types in Baltimore regarded us as lightweights or worse. Thus, one night in the summer of 1970, the *Harry* collective was invaded by some twenty-five blithering

Maoists armed with large sticks. They called themselves, and I'm not making this up, the "Balto Cong." They claimed they were liberating the paper in the name of "the people." In vain we tried to tell them that the only thing the people were going to get by liberating *Harry* was ten thousand dollars in debt and a mouse-infested row house with overdue rent.

There were about eight *Harry* staffers in the office that evening. The Balto Cong held us prisoner all night and subjected each of us to individual "consciousness-raising" sessions. You'd be hauled off to another room where ten or a dozen of these nutcakes would sit in a circle and scream that you were a revisionist running dog imperialist paper tiger whatchama-thing. I don't know about the rest of the staff, but I conceded as quick as I could to every word they said.

Finally, about 6:00 A.M., we mollified the Balto Cong by agreeing to set up a "people's committee" to run the paper. It would be made up of their group and our staff. We would all meet that night on neutral turf at the Free Clinic. The Balto Cong left in triumph. My airhead girlfriend had been converted to Maoism during her consciousness-raising session. And she left with them.

While the Balto Cong went home to take throat pastilles and make new sticks or what-

ever, we rolled into action. There were, in those days, about a hundred burned-out "street people" who depended on peddling *Harry* for their livelihood. We rallied all of these, including several members of a friendly motorcycle gang, and explained to them how little sales appeal *Harry* would have if it were filled with quotations from Ho Chi Minh instead of free-love personals. They saw our point. Then we phoned the Balto Cong crash pad and told them we were ready for the meeting. "But," we said, "is the Free Clinic large enough to hold us all?" "What do you mean?" they said. "Well," we said, "we're bringing about a hundred of our staff members and there's, what, twenty-five of you, so..." They said, um, they'd get back to us.

We were by no means sure the Balto Cong threat had abated. Therefore, the staff photographer, whom I'll call Bob, and I were set to guard the *Harry* household. Bob and I were the only two people on the staff who owned guns. Bob was an ex-Marine and something of a flop as a hippie. He could never get the hair and the clothes right and preferred beer to pot. But he was very enthusiastic about hippie girls. Bob still had his service automatic. I had a little .22 caliber pistol that I'd bought in a fit of wild self-dramatization during the '68 riots. "You never know when the heavy shit is going to come down," I had been fond of saying. Although I'd pictured it "coming down" more from the Richard Nixon than the Balto Cong direction. Anyway, Bob and I stood guard. We stood anxious guard every night for two weeks, which seemed an immense length of time back in 1970. Of course, we began to get slack, not to say stoned, and forgot things like locking the front door. And through that front door, at the end of two weeks, came a half dozen hulking Balto Cong. Bob and I were at the back of the first-floor office. Bob had his pistol in the waistband of his ill-fitting bell-bottoms. He went to fast draw and, instead, knocked the thing down the front of his pants. My pistol was in the top drawer of a desk. I reached in and grabbed it, but I was so nervous that I got my thigh in front of the desk drawer and couldn't get my hand with the pistol in it out. I yanked like mad but I was stuck. I was faced with a terrible dilemma. I could either let go of the pistol and pull my hand out of the drawer or I could keep hold of the pistol and leave my hand stuck in there. It never occurred to me to move my leg.

The invading Balto Cong were faced with one man fishing madly in his crotch and another apparently being eaten by a desk. It stopped them cold. As they stood perplexed, I was struck by an inspiration. It was a wooden desk, I would simply fire through it. I flipped the safety off the .22, pointed the barrel at the Balto Cong and was just curling my finger around the trigger when the Maoists parted and there, in the line of fire, stood my airhead ex-girlfriend. "I've come to get my ironing board and my Hermann Hesse novels," she said, and led her companions upstairs to our former bedroom.

"It's a trap!" said Bob, extracting his gun from the bottom of a pants leg. When the Balto Cong and the ex-girlfriend came back downstairs they faced two exceedingly wide-eyed guys crouching like leopards behind an impromptu barricade of overturned book cases. They sped for the exit.

It turned out later that Bob was an under-cover cop. He'd infiltrated the Harry collective shortly after the first issue. All his photos had been developed at the police laboratory. We'd wondered why every time we got busted for marijuana the case was dropped. Bob would always go to the District Attorney's office and convince them a trial would "blow his cover." It was important for him to remain undetected so he could keep his eye on... well, on a lot of hippie girls. Bob was in no rush to get back to the Grand Theft Auto detail.

I eventually read some of the reports Bob filed with the police department. They were made up of " ...is involved in the *Harry* 'scene' primarily as a means of upsetting his parents who are socially prominent," and other such. Today, Bob is an insurance investigator in Baltimore. He's still friends with the old *Harry* staff. And, of the whole bunch of us, I believe there's only one who's far enough to the left to even be called a Democrat.

WHAT I BELIEVE NOW

Nothing. Well, nothing much. I mean, I believe things that can be proven by reason and by experiment, and, believe you me, I want to see the logic and the lab equipment. I believe that Western civilization, after some disgusting glitches, has become almost civilized. I believe it is our second duty to improve it. I believe it is our third duty to extend it if we can. But let's be careful about that last point. Not everybody is ready to be civilized. I wasn't in 1969.

Philosophy

Training a Horse

by Daniel Pinkwater

"Before we start, I think Sumo wrestling is a rotten way to choose Top Pet."

Once, Jill acquired a mare in bad condition – starving. The vet instructed us to gradually increase the feed, and exercise the mare – most important. The exercise consisted of holding one end of a long line, attached to the mare's halter, and snapping a long whip behind her, not touching her, to make her walk in a circle. One should speak encouragingly to the horse, the horse book said. I'd had a lot of experience training dogs. How different could this be?

I got the hang of it. So did the horse. She was weak and tired, and reluctant to move, but I got her moving. I kept chatting and snapping the whip. She kept moving. After some days, I hardly had to snap the whip. She was responding to my chatter, and she was showing improvement. I was gratified, and sincere in my praise.

But the rehabilitation went on for a long time. Twice a day, for a whole hour, I worked with her. I was glad to see her progress, but I was getting bored. My mind started to wander.

Came a day when I was a million miles away. I was sending the mare in her circles automatically. Talking it up, robotically. I did not notice in time to react when she stepped into the center of the circle, put a hind foot on my boot, bumped me with her hip, sending me to the ground, and stood on my leg, firmly.

"There's a horse standing on me," I thought. "This is what it's like when a horse stands on you."

Callahan

He's licking his balls right now- can I have him call you?

Distributed by Levin Represents

WE CAN'T AFFORD TO SEND YOU BOTH TO OBEDIENCE SCHOOL, SO WE'RE GOING TO SEND ONE OF YOU, AND HAVE HIM TEACH THE OTHER.

© CHRONICLE FEATURES 1994 · 2/15

It seemed like a long time before the mare took her weight off my leg, and I was able to scramble to my feet... foot. I remembered not to assess whether my leg was injured or broken before hopping around in front of her and punching her in the brisket as hard as I could. This had to be settled on the spot, or I'd have no more influence with her at all.

My leg was not broken – hardly bruised. She took her punch philosophically. She looked me in the eye, calmly. I knew what she meant to convey: "Pay attention. And don't speak to me as if I were some puppydog. Tell me a lie, and you will deserve whatever you get."

We were best friends for the rest of her life.

Whenever you get too busy,
THINK OF ANTS.
Ants are the busiest creatures of all.
Yet they can always find time
to go on a picnic.

Quote Repair

by Flash Rosenberg

I've always loved quotes. Quotes concisely package thoughts so much neater than it ever feels just mumbling through the gabby confusion of life. Not religion, but a well-turned phrase is the only thing (well okay, besides sex or food) that gives me some sense of Universal Truth. But over time, many old proverbs have grown a bit shabby. Out of touch. Their wit has wilted. But with a little heckling and tweaking, the following standard platitudes have been repaired by playing "Quote Doctor."

Idleness is the holiday of fools.
— CHESTERFIELD
• *quote repair* •
HOLIDAYS FOOL US INTO
IDLENESS.

Wit is the salt of conversation, not the food.
— HAZLETT
• *quote repair* •
FOOD CAUSES WITLESS
CONVERSATION ABOUT SALT.

The lovers of freedom will be free.
— BURKE
• *quote repair* •
THE FREEDOM OF LOVERS WILL
BE EXPENSIVE.

It is better to bend than break.
— FRENCH PROVERB
• *quote repair* •
IT IS BETTER TO TAKE A BREAK.

A delay is better than a disaster.
— ANONYMOUS
• *quote repair* •
IT'S NO DISASTER TO
GET LAID.

"Waste is a terrible thing to mind."

The cautious seldom err.
— CONFUCIUS
• *quote repair* •
THE ERRONEOUS ARE SELDOM
CAUGHT.

Innocence is ashamed of nothing.
— ROUSSEAU
• *quote repair add* •
...EXCEPT ITS INNOCENCE.

Catch the bear before you sell
his skin.
— ANONYMOUS
• *quote repair* •
YOU'LL CATCH HELL IF YOU BARE
YOUR SKIN.

All work and no play makes Jack a dull boy.
— ENGLISH PROVERB
• *quote repair* •
DULL WORK AND NO BOYS
MAKES ONE JACK-OFF.

The journey of 1,000 miles begins with one step.
— LAO TZE
• *quote repair add* •
...AND THE SINGING OF 1,000 BOTTLES
OF BEER ON THE WALL.

The gift of a bad man can bring no good.
— EURIPIDES
• *quote repair* •
BRING ME THE GIFT OF A GOOD
MAN TO MAKE ME BAD.

If you keep saying things are going to be bad,
you have a good chance of being a prophet.
— ISAAC BASHEVIS SINGER
• *quote repair* •
IF YOU KEEP SAYING YOU NEED A
PROFIT, YOU HAVE A GOOD CHANCE
OF DOING BAD THINGS.

Friendship is the band of reason.
— SHERIDAN
• *quote repair* •
REASONABLE FRIENDS DON'T
START A BAND.

We are less convinced by what we hear
than what we see.
— EURIPIDES
• *quote repair add* •
...AND WE SEE EVEN LESS
WHEN WE'RE ALREADY
CONVINCED.

No duty is more urgent than that
of returning thanks.
— ST. AMBROSE
• *quote repair* •
NO URGE IS MORE DIRTY
THAN THAT OF
REGURGITATING DRINKS.

Happy are those who have no doubt
of themselves.
— FLAUBERT
• *quote repair* •
STUPID ARE THOSE WHO HAVE
NO DOUBT OF THEMSELVES.

If I Live in a Fantasy World, Why Do I Have to Pay Taxes?

by Rita Rudner

With a visit from the same luck fairy who visits teenagers who get pregnant the first time they have sex, I got audited the first time I ever filed. No one ever really prepared me for the paperwork that accompanies adulthood. Someone in the show I was in had mentioned that you had to save receipts and take them to an accountant before April 15. I kept them all in a big shoebox and brought them to an accountant on the fourteenth. They were in no particular order. I just dumped them on the accountant's desk and expected him to do something magical.

He said, "You haven't put these receipts in categories and added them up?"

I said, "Isn't that your job?" I sounded like a smart aleck, but I really thought that's what accountants did.

He said, "Why don't you go home and put these in little piles and add them up?"

I said, "Because I'm a dancer. If I could put things in little piles and add them up, I'd be an accountant."

I can still see the hatred in his eyes. I sat in

For accountant Ted Gribble, appearing on the hit show "CPA Unplugged" was a dream come true.

the outer office and made little receipt piles for hours. I added them up to the best of my more than limited ability because I didn't have a calculator and I thought if I asked him for his, he might hit me. I gave him a sheet of numbers I had partially made up, and a few weeks later he sent me papers to sign and send in. Since I'd been on the road for almost a year and I

God gets audited.

"YOU OWE TAXES FROM A PREVIOUS LIFE."

had quite a few deductions, a few months later I got a five-hundred dollar refund from the government. I thought, "This is good."

I spent the five hundred dollars frivolously on food and rent, and one day a letter arrived from the IRS. I didn't really understand it, something about going downtown on June 12 and bringing my records. I thought, "Maybe the IRS is inviting me to provide music." I called my accountant and told him about my letter. There was a long silence and he said, "I'm too busy to help you. Bring all the receipts you brought to me down to the IRS and act innocent."

Act innocent? Innocent of what? I called one of my friends and told her what had happened.

"You're going down yourself? You're not even bringing a lawyer?" she gasped.

"Why would I need a lawyer? I haven't done anything wrong," I said innocently.

"Well, you've got the innocent act down," she said.

On the twelfth of June I took the subway to Rectum Street or whatever it was called, took a number, and sat in the waiting room with all of my shoeboxes. Sweat was in the air. There were lots of nervous people sitting around me holding their numbers. I didn't blame them for being nervous. I'd be nervous too if I didn't have the shoeboxes. I was confident that everything was going to be all right, although the sobbing noises that were coming from behind the dirty glass doors were not comforting.

Finally, my number was called. I stood up and said, "I'll have a half pound of very lean roast beef and some potato salad." I got a laugh in the auditing room at the IRS. (This was a sign that ten years later I would become a comedian.) I walked into the little cubbyhole of the poor bespectacled little man who had been assigned to my case and put all of my shoeboxes on his desk.

He said, "Why did you bring me shoes?"

I said, "These are my receipts." I opened the boxes, and because of the subway journey and because I had not stapled any of the piles together, they were back in their original state of chaos.

We sat there for eight hours. This guy was thorough. He was so thorough, he found some mistakes. He found a whole pile of receipts that were deductions I had forgotten to include. There were sobbing noises coming from my cubbyhole and they weren't coming from me. At the end of the audit, the IRS owed me two hundred dollars.

I wish I could say I've gotten better at paperwork through the years, but all I can say is that I no longer use shoeboxes to hold my receipts. I've switched to paper bags.

"PLEASE EXIT THROUGH HERE, SIR, TO MAKE SURE YOU DON'T HAVE ANY MONEY LEFT."

"I assume you can produce receipts for all this money you claim to have given the poor."

A Pet Rabbit and the Call Of the Stepfather

by David Scott

"NO SHEDDING!"

I once saw an upright piano fall off a fish dock into a boat hold full of freshly caught flounder. I was perhaps 12 years old on vacation in a remote fishing village in Nova Scotia. The men had obviously moved the piano by boat from someone's home across the bay, but on its way down the dock it got away from them and fell into the mass of flounder. It made a sound that I will never forget.

I associate this sound for some reason with my experience as a stepfather. Perhaps because of the near insanity and the absurdity of the vision. Or maybe it was the chaos of the joining together of such inharmonious objects like fish and piano, much like the chaos and insanity that occurs when creating a family from things like divorce, alimony, and mom's new dork of a boyfriend.

The only daughter of the woman I loved was 13 years old. Her name was Nikki. A classic struggle for the favor of her mother began between us. Nikki didn't really like me at first, I once tried to teach her to play tennis and she kept complaining that I was "not hitting the balls to where she was standing." And she called me a "dork" a lot and refused to be seen with me in public and did all the other little things that the stepchild/stepparent relationship seems to require.

Anyway, one day she wanted a rabbit. I never believed she really wanted a rabbit; it could have been anything, giraffe, hippo, ocelot. I think she just wanted an animal of some sort as a kind of parenting test for us. And so she got a rabbit.

It was a hideous little white furred lump, an angora rabbit, highly prized in some areas of the world for its sweaters. It moved with a slow kind of geriatric hop every once in a while and chewed on things constantly. It really couldn't help the chewing part, I later learned: it had to chew things all its life or else its teeth would grow through its brain or some such thing.

I offered to build a cage for the rabbit, to which my stepdaughter responded that if it was going to have to live in a cage then there was no real sense to having it at all. And so the rabbit "ran wild" through the house. Although it didn't really run, but just slowly hopped about aimlessly from room to room, peeing every once in a while.

The next weekend I was watching a football game. It was a close game and in the fourth quarter as they were lining up to try a tying field goal that would send the game into overtime, the picture suddenly disappeared and was replaced by that familiar evil blizzard-like hiss of static and meaningless blurred dots.

The rabbit had eaten through the antenna wire.

In the days that followed, the rabbit ate through the phone wire so often that communication with the outside world became nearly impossible. Phone lines were spliced so short that you could only raise the receiver a few inches once it rang. It ate the plugs off radio cords and lamps and seemed to have developed a special taste for the exotic three-pronged extension cord plug. Every day I would find new eaten wires. We wrapped them in tinfoil (my wife's idea), yet still it went on.

One day I came home to find my wife sitting on the couch with a riding crop that she would use to prod the rabbit away from the walls where the outlets and the wires were each time it moved in that direction. That was a turning point for me – I heard that sound of piano on fish. We demanded that the rabbit be in a cage, or else.

Luckily for us, the rabbit (Fred was his name) ate through a phone line during one of Nikki's romantic type calls, and so the next day he was living in a cage outside. It was a nice cage – it had an opening door where he could hop out and explore the world to the end of his tether, which was about ten feet of rope.

I was at home alone on the couch one Saturday, I think the women may have been out shopping, when, out of the corner of my eye, I noticed the rabbit hopping by the sliding glass doors near the rear of our house.

Fred has eaten through his tether, I thought, and no doubt he will now wander into the woods to be eaten by a predator. How cruel yet wonderful are the ways of nature.

Yet deep within me I could feel the guilt growing like some malignant seed. I could see her mother's stern and sexless look, as Nikki screamed, "He killed my rabbit, Mom!" There was no way out of it – they would blame me forever. I left the couch and set out to capture the rabbit with my bare hands.

For some reason I thought I might be able to just walk to the rabbit and pick it up. This did not happen – instead, the rabbit would allow me to get near enough to it, but when I reached for it, it would hop just out of my grasp. We did this "rabbit shuffle" around the house twice when finally I just tried to throw myself at it. It hopped a safe distance away and made those little nose twitching movements at me. I had the feeling it was laughing at me.

I slowly pulled myself to my feet and gave a cold stare to my prey. Playtime was over. I stretched, took a deep breath, and shot after

him at full speed. At first it seemed as though I was gaining on him but then he began moving at a slightly faster hop. I was on my knees after a few laps around the house, gasping for air. The rabbit was just out of reach, waiting, no doubt, for me to catch my breath.

It was then that I saw the stick. It was a long stick with half a dozen small twigs on the end that made it a kind of rake. I thought perhaps if I could get a part of the stick in front of it, it would run back towards me, and I would have it. Tool use goes hand in hand with intelligence, as you know.

I actually managed to get the twigged end of the stick in front of it on my first try, but instead of running back towards me it just ran around it. After a few more laps around the house with the stick, I lost control. I began shouting at the rabbit and calling it names. I stopped and threw stones at it. I chased it like a madman, swinging at it with the stick, hoping to send it into orbit. I cursed it, its family, its sweaters; I tried to sneak up on it with bigger sticks, I threw the sticks like spears, I may have fallen a few times but I don't remember, and sometime later I found myself wheezing on my knees with the rabbit a stick's length away. It was drinking from a small puddle of water.

Slowly, as my breathing returned to normal, a small light began to grow dimly in the recesses of my blood-lusting, rabbit-maddened brain. The theme music from the movie 2001 began to play somewhere. I went inside, got a small saucer of water and a carrot. The rabbit watched me as I put them in its cage. It hopped inside, and I closed the door.

We discovered after that to use a chain to tether the rabbit. It looked a little odd, this rabbit, who had originally been the champion of freedom of movement, dragging a length of dogchain around after him like he was some kind of dangerous felon of rabbithood.

Nikki gradually forgot about Fred and then one day I came home to find his chain stretched out on the ground and just a white tuft of fur left near the end of it. Fred was gone but the memory and the sound of fallen pianos on flounder live on.

Psychology

Carolyn sensed another mood change coming on.

Quitters Never Win

by Susan Shapiro

"WHATTAYA SAY, KID....
WHICH ONE'S THE GUY
WHO KILLED YOUR DAD?"

DAY 1: Wake up and put on nicotine patch to once and for all quit pack-a-day habit. Write a list of reasons: Live 15 years longer, have healthy children, be socially acceptable. Tear up list and make better one: Look younger, have fewer wrinkles, get more dates, spite enemies. Decide to go out and buy carrots, celery, gum, orange juice, fruit, sugar-free lollipops and rice cakes. Eat it all by 11 A.M., desperately craving cigarette. Try to work. Instead take all-day nap. Have a drink later with old boyfriend Peter, who says, "Kissing a smoker is like licking a dirty ash-tray," then drinks seven beers and a Cognac and comes on to me. Actually consider it, but can't face sex without a cigarette later. At 2 A.M., go out and purchase three packages of fat-free Entenmann's brownies.

DAY 2: Wake up sick from brownies and cold caught walking 14 blocks to get them at 2 A.M. Put on patch. Buy Sudafed. Take two. Feel better. Feel delirious. Take a nap. Try to work, but can't concentrate on anything but wanting to smoke. One hour on exercise bike: Oprah's "Mothers Who Want Their Kids Taken Away" puts problem into perspective.

Read that schizophrenics and manic-depressives in mental hospitals commit sui-cide when their cigarettes are taken away. Decide never to have children. Ask brother, the doctor, for 65 more patches. Take another Sudafed. Is there a Sudafed group in the city?

DAY 3: Put on patch. Have breakfast with friend Vern, who says that after he quit smok-ing, his concentration didn't come back for two years. Scan obits for people who died of lung cancer and feel happy when they're in their 50's. Take a nap, dream I'm smoking and feel sad that I went off the wagon. Wake up and find I'm not but want to be. Take 100 deep

ZIPPY   "SMOKE AND MIRRORS"   BILL GRIFFITH

THE BOYS ARE SUDDENLY BIT BY TH' CIGAR CRAZE..

MMMM... NOTHING LIKE AN ILLEGALLY IMPORTED "PAR-TAGAS" CUBAN!

ITS ILLICIT AROMA & DARK, SUPPLE LEAF ARE INDEED MUY FABULOSO!

I DON'T KNOW... THIS "DON LINO" TORPEDO FROM HONDURAS WAS AGED SIX MONTHS IN A FLOOR-TO-CEILING CEDAR-LINED AGING ROOM!

YEHHH... LOVE THIS "MACANDO" PRINCE PHILIP WITH TH' CONNECTICUT SHADE-GROWN WRAPPER!

MMM... I COULD FONDLE MY BURL GLOSS HUMIDOR FOR HOURS.. DID I TELL YOU IT'S TONGUE-IN-GROOVE?

YEH, BUT IS IT FELT-BOTTOMED FOR THAT TOUCH OF ELEGANCE!

TH' QUEASINESS RISES EVER SO GRADUALLY FROM TH' STOMACH AND SMOOTHLY ENVELOPES TH' HEAD & EXTREMITIES..

NAUSEA.. ..IT SIMPLY CANNOT BE RUSHED!!

breaths. Breathing is overrated. Take a walk and count how many stores on the blocks sell cigarettes. Get more patches in mail from brother, along with pictures of cancerous tumors. Try to work. See a movie with Peter in which all actors smoke. Eat two buckets of popcorn. Peter says: "My cousin Janet quit in three days on Nicorettes. Try Nicorettes," though I told him I tried them and threw up, then went out and smoked two packs to get the taste out of my mouth. Don't invite him in. Read that nicotine's harder to quit than heroin. Take another Sudafed.

DAY 4: Put on patch. Think of smoking. Brother calls to say don't even think of smoking with patch on, someone's fingers fell off. Lunch with Andrea, who coughed every time I took out a cigarette for 15 years but now says, "I can't hang out with you when you're like this, you're too intense." Bump into old colleague Dave, who quit smoking and gained 29 pounds in four months but thinks it was the smart choice. Consider heroin. Try to work but realize it's impossible to be a freelance writer, a nonsmoker and thin in the same year.

MY FIRST NICOTINE PATCH

Sudafed losing its bite, check into Comtrex. Negotiate self-destructive behaviors: decide that taking sleeping pill, smoking a joint, getting drunk or having sex with Peter one more time is better than a Marlboro or Oreos, though not if done on the same night.

DAY 5: Put on patch. Feel depressed and

edgy, sweating. Hand shaking while reading the paper, where tobacco company executives say nicotine isn't addictive. Buy a pacifier, pretending it's a cool rap toy, wondering why anyone expects morality from the people who plastered penis-faced camels all over the country. Think of ten 70-year-old smokers still alive. Dinner with novelist friend Kathy, who chain-smokes in my face while saying she thinks it's great that I'm quitting. On the way home, try to buy a 25-cent loosie (loose cigarette) at local bodega but guy thinks I'm cigarette police. Take it as an omen. Try to think of one famous writer who doesn't drink or smoke.

DAY 6: Put patch on. Walk around city chewing. Do high-impact aerobics for three hours. Walk out of health club wanting cigarette. Stare at people smoking and wonder why they look so beautiful and happy. Think of money I'm saving from not smoking. Spend $46 on seven boxes of fat-free cookies, 27 cinnamon sticks and three Lean Cuisines. Snap rubber band around wrist 100 times. My father, an oncologist, says, "You'll never do it," forgetting that when he quit his 35-year three-pack-a-day habit he gained 35 pounds and smoked a six-inch cigar every night. Decide neurosis is genetic. On stationary bike watch "Saturday Night Live," which quotes tobacco company execs saying that the 400,000 annual smoking-related deaths aren't really dead. Neighbor complains bike makes too much noise. Do serenity exercises. Picture sitting on a tropical beach, where I'm happily smoking.

DAY 7: Put on patch. Have brunch with Peter, who says, while drinking six margaritas, that I've gained weight and need to learn more self-control. Make note to quit Peter. Read article about Bosnia, noticing only that soldier in picture is smoking. Eat more celery, fruit, salad. Polish off Oreos. Feel sick and bloated, dying for cigarette. Take off patch. Run outside. Bum cigarette from homeless person, who lights it. Puff slowly. Feel happy for the

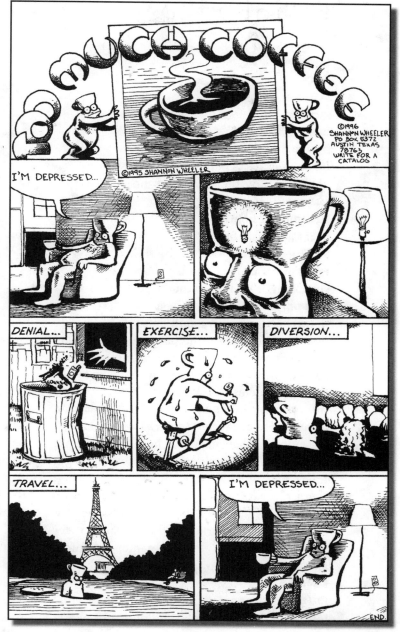

first time in six days. Stop coughing, calm down. Finish two articles. Go back outside, offer same guy $2 for two more cigarettes. Smoke them quickly. Feel nauseated, dizzy. Bump into Vern and Andrea, who say: "We were just coming by to say how proud we are that you haven't smoked in a week! Congratulations!" Feel guilty, defeated. Drink bottle of wine by myself. Fall asleep on couch with clothes on.

DAY 1: Wake up and put on nicotine patch once and for all...

Bright Ideas #1: Keep It Moving

by Harry Shearer

It's not easy being a person who, judging by the scores on those old career counseling tests in college, just likes to help people. I'm speaking, as it happens, of myself.

The urge to be of assistance to mankind isn't something a guy can switch on or off like so much electrified anti-burglar fencing. It's a habit of mind, like looking for stuff on sale.

When I talk about helping my fellow man, don't get me wrong. You won't find me down on Skid Row scooping out mashed potatoes for the homeless on Thanksgiving. Not that I think that's a bad thing to do. It's just that I can never figure out where to park down there.

My particular version of help takes a more cerebral form: I can't avoid thinking of Bright Ideas that would make all our lives easier, more pleasant, more healthful. Unlike those inventors who make a fortune in late-night TV commercials by marketing their ideas, I prefer to give mine away. It's just neater and nicer and means I have to spend less time talking to lawyers.

Bright Ideas are common sense notions that just seem to have eluded the notice of everyone else. For example, ozone.

Don't worry. I'm not going to leave you there, with just the word ozone dangling over your breakfast like so much unshredded wheat. Ozone is believed to be hazardous to human health when present in large enough quantities at ground level, where humans tend to live. But there's equal concern about the depletion of the ozone layer up in the stratosphere, where it protects us from cancer-causing solar rays.

You see what I'm getting at? Too much ozone down here because of cars and things. Too little ozone up there presumably because of profligate use of our man-size chemistry sets. We could change our entire way of life, which even the most Calvinist of environmentalists may, in their more reflective moments, realize is a pathetic pipe dream. Or we can figure out a way to pump the excess ozone away from down here and pipe or spray or dump it up there. Turn the bad ozone into good ozone, beat our smog into plowshares, that sort of thing.

Don't ask me about specifics. That's for the drones to figure out. I just know that if there's too much of it here and not enough of it there, that's the kind of problem man can solve.

Same with water. Not only do we live in a desert in Southern California, but our desert is also going through a drought – a pretty classic case of not enough water. Historically, our policy has been to con, buy, or steal water from some part of Northern California that can't afford good enough legal advice, but those folks are, sadly, getting wise to us.

On the other hand, there are parts of the country, like Louisiana, that are so water-logged that they must constantly build and reinforce dikes and levees and other temporary defenses against the inexorable watery onslaught. As it happens, Louisiana is connected to our corner of the world by a pipeline, whose function is to transport natural gas to our ovens and water heaters. But it's a pipeline, just the same. Therein the Bright Idea. Flush out the pipeline periodically and use it to send Mississippi River water straight to our thirsty little settlement.

Using a gas pipeline to transport drinking water is no more disgusting than some of the things we do now, like using the same trucks to transport food in one direction and hazardous wastes in the other. Making the process even less disgusting is a job for the experts. The nub of the idea is simplicity itself: Louisiana is dirt-poor; we're aerospace- and movie-rich. Let's make a deal. Then we can tell the Northern Californians to take their water and stick it in their sulfite-loaded wines.

One more dose of help for a harried humanity. What slows down freeway traffic almost as much as accidents themselves are the remains of mishaps: cars crumpled into the median dividers, CHiPs setting out flares on the shoulder, firefighters hosing down flaming former Toyotas. Drivers slow down to check out the debris; other drivers plow into their taillights; the great chain of freeway disaster is renewed. Rubbernecking at fender-benders, as the traffic jocks put it, is an easily preventable hazard.

All we have to do, Bright Idea-wise, is equip all California Highway Patrol cars with folding screens – the kind used to partition hospital rooms, for example. So the first thing the officers do at the scene of an accident is set up the screen, shielding the debris from view. Passing drivers no longer see broken glass, revolving red lights and mashed fenders; all they see is the screens, perhaps blank, perhaps emblazoned with helpful slogans like "Keep moving; show's over." I don't know. Again, I'm not a detail man. I'm doing big-picture work here.

There are, of course, plenty more Bright Ideas where these came from. But I'm running out of space. Besides, a guy gets tired trying to help all the time. Now I know how Mother Teresa felt.

THIS MODERN WORLD by TOM TOMORROW

ACCORDING TO NASA SCIENTISTS, THE OZONE LAYER REACHED RECORD LEVELS OF DEPLETION THIS SUMMER...YOU PROBABLY DIDN'T HEAR ABOUT IT THOUGH, SINCE NASA--FEARFUL OF A POLITICAL BACKLASH FROM RIGHT-WING ACTIVISTS--CHOSE TO DOWNPLAY THE INFORMATION...

HEH, HEH...IT'S REALLY NO BIG DEAL...

YOU JUST MIGHT WANT TO USE A SUNBLOCK WITH A SLIGHTLY HIGHER SUN PROTECTION FACTOR...

LIKE ABOUT 100...

APPARENTLY THESE ACTIVISTS WOULD RATHER RISK THE HEALTH OF EVERY LIVING BEING ON THE PLANET THAN ADMIT THE POSSIBILITY OF A PROBLEM...RUSH LIMBAUGH LEADS THE CHARGE, VOCIFEROUSLY DENYING THE VERY EXISTENCE OF A HOLE IN THE OZONE...

HEY--ALL THOSE SCIENTISTS HAVE ARE A BUNCH OF INSTRUMENTS AND MEASUREMENTS!

I HAVE AN IDEOLOGY!

EIB EXTREMISM IN BROADCASTING

MAYBE HE'S RIGHT--BUT WHAT IF HE'S WRONG? AFTER ALL, WE'RE OPERATING ON A PRETTY SLIM MARGIN OF ERROR HERE...

THIN BAND OF ATMOSPHERE--SUPPORTING LIFE AS WE KNOW IT...

INFINITE REACHES OF SPACE--RATHER LESS HOSPITABLE TO LIFE AS WE KNOW IT...

BUT WHO KNOWS--MAYBE SOME PEOPLE SEE THE DESTRUCTION OF THE OZONE LAYER AS NOTHING MORE THAN A POSSIBLE NEW GROWTH INDUSTRY...

HEY FRANK--NICE ENVIRONMENTAL SUIT! THAT'S THE NEW FORD MODEL, ISN'T IT?

YOU BET! MARGE AND I ALWAYS BUY AMERICAN!

Relationships

"At this time we'd like to board passengers who are single men between the ages of 25 and 36."

"YOUR DEPTH IS TOO DEEP FOR ME!"

LUST IN SPACE

SAFE SEX

ORGY OF HANDS

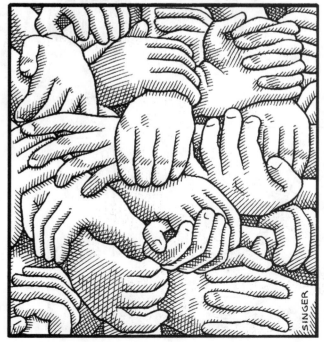

Wake Up and Find the Coffee

by Ian Shoales

Last week I went into a coffee house to get, you know, a cup of coffee, only to be told that actual coffee was unavailable. Would I like a tasty cappuccino, cafe au lait, or espresso? A double decaf latte with one of those little Italian biscuits that tastes like chalk? They had those, but a steaming java, a plain ordinary cup of joe? No way.

This mutant coffee thing is getting out of hand. It's even hard to get a cuppa mud at the local convenience store. It used to be simple: Get large paper container, put under urn tap, pour, attach appropriate lid, pay and go. Today, convenience stores all have an Isle Du Cawfay or some damn thing: it offers cinnamon coffee, vanilla coffee and decaf Viennese, from beans fresh-squeezed by formerly Soviet virgins. I'm not against this stuff, but it's not what I look for in liquefied caffeine; I want a blister on my lips and a knot in my stomach. I want my coffee black, bitter and scalding.

Give me that little pleasure, America. I promise I won't sue you.

Alas, we're well on the road to tepid exoticism. Have you tried to find vanilla ice cream at the grocery store lately? You could get frostbite from rummaging. You have to claw your way past Wally Walnut Peanut Brittle Supreme, or Cherry Brownie Fudge Syrup Surprise, ice cream with so much extra junk crammed into its mass it looks like a tub of frozen glue with chunks of bark floating in it. If you find vanilla ice cream at all, it's usually Milli Vanilla Whole Bean Rain Forest Saver, with vanilla beans suspended in its depths like boulders in a glacier.

While we're on the subject, isn't it time to declare a moratorium on microbreweries? Walk into an upscale tavern these days, and there's a 12-foot wall of bottles behind the bar, floor to ceiling. If you ask the bartender what kind of beers they serve, you'll die of thirst before he reaches the end of the list. And all the names have the same kind of annoying, vaguely macho ring to them: Ugly Alligator Ale, or One-Eyed Pete's Pale Porter. I'll go mad, I tell you! Mad!

"You bought unscented deodorant, non-alcoholic beer and decaffeinated coffee. Why'd you even bother going?"

We've got to nip this thing in the bud, my friends. We're on the road to a world where we'll be able to flavor our foods with cumin, curry, or cilantro, but not salt. We used to drink water from the tap, remember that? Then we switched to bubbly water from foreign lands; now it has to be cherry-flavored bubbly water, or we won't touch it.

We have special shampoos for our individual hair needs. We need special outfits to ride a damn bicycle. We have call waiting, call forwarding, caller i.d. — but when's the last time you actually talked to a human being on the telephone?

Our new culture is all quarters, no pennies, prayer in school but no education, all croissants and no doughnuts. We're not smoking! Tomatoes will stay ripe for centuries.

We welcome space aliens, but not illegal ones. (As if Martians carry work visas.) We used to shoot tin cans from stumps with .22s. Today we shoot each other with .357s. We used to drive gas-guzzlers, guilt-free; today we drive little tiny cars with strange names not found in nature. Do we really feel better about ourselves? Of course we don't.

We're just trying to prove that we can control our appetites. "I don't have a sugar jones," we say to the world, "I just have a sudden craving for Huggy-Buggy Sweet 'N' Sticky Health Bars. That's all."

I don't want to alarm you (well, OK, I do), but it seems like we're ripe for an invasion. Lean and hungry barbarians from the east, take note. You won't even

"I SEE TOAST IS MAKING A COMEBACK."

need weapons. All you need are basic goods: sugar, salt, coffee, tea, whole milk, alcohol, red meat, tobacco. I don't want to sound like a traitor, but we're pushovers... I gotta go.

TROUBLE AT THE 'SMART DRINK' BAR..

OK, PAL, I'M CUTTING YOU OFF... YOU'VE HAD ENOUGH!

© 1992 NORMAN DOG

The "Dear Mom" Form Letter

by Roger Simon

Do you think anyone saves love letters anymore? Does anyone still tie them up in a ribbon and tuck them away in an attic trunk to be savored years later?

I am betting they do not.

And I am betting this because I don't think anybody writes love letters anymore. Or any other kind of meaningful personal letter.

When the PBS series "The Civil War" was popular a few years ago, viewers were amazed at the high quality of the letters and personal journals written by the soldiers of that era.

Many of these soldiers had little formal schooling – much less schooling than a young person would receive today – yet they wrote with a clarity and eloquence that verged on the poetic.

How is it that these simple people came to have these skills?

They had to have them. They lived in an age when the letter was the chief form of long-distance communication. Letters were necessary to conduct one's life and business. And, more important, to keep in touch with

one's relatives. (For people of earlier eras, keeping in touch with family was a serious obligation as well as a considerable joy. Today, even though communication is effortless, it is viewed as neither.)

And because people knew you by how you wrote, letters were taken seriously.

They were saved. They were pressed into Bibles, kept in albums, tied up with ribbons and stored in chests and trunks.

The power of the written message has not disappeared. Every time a company adopts an e-mail system on its computers, it discovers the same thing: People would rather write short messages to each other than speak on the phone.

But even though this short-form electronic communication is a kind of writing, it rarely is eloquent. If you have ever monitored electronic "chat" groups, you are instantly struck by how rudimentary (to say nothing of rude) most of the communication is.

And I doubt that many people print out their e-mail, tie it in a ribbon and save it in a trunk in the attic.

There is a solution to this. I found it the other day. And it still gives me chills.

In its best-selling word processing program called "Word for Windows 95," Microsoft has included many pre-written forms and letters. All you have to do is plug in a name and address.

Most of these letters are for business, but one of them is labeled "Letter to Mom."

Dear Mom, it begins. *How are you doing? Everything is fine with me!*

I'm sorry that I haven't written for a while, but I've been really busy! As you know, I really like computers, and I'm spending long hours in front of a screen both at work and at home.

In fact, I just bought a great program. It's really neat — a collection of business letters that I can customize any way I want. For example, there's a letter to people who are late paying their bills and another one that complains about a defective product.

I'm sure it'll save me a lot of time and energy — you know how hard it is for me to write letters! Now I'll be able to think about business instead of worrying about what to say in letters.

Too bad they don't have one for writing to you! Ha ha ha. They should also have one for thanking Aunt Patty for the cookies! Nah — form letters could never replace the personal touch!

Gotta run now, Mom! All my love!

I am sure the folks at Microsoft conceived this as a joke. I am sure Bill Gates would never send this letter to his mom or seriously want anybody to just plug in some new names and send it to their relatives.

But I wonder how many people actually have sent out this letter? How many people have sunk this low?

So why am I reprinting the letter if I deplore it?

I am doing it as a public service.

Because if you ever get this letter from a loved one, I want to give you plenty of time to change your will.

Religion

THE SEVEN DAYS OF CREATION BY D. CODOR ©

FIRST DAY · SECOND DAY · THIRD DAY

FOURTH DAY · FIFTH DAY · SIXTH DAY · SEVENTH DAY

BLAMER.

YO AMERICANS! DON'T WALLOW IN EXISTENTIAL ANGST WHEN YOU CAN SHOP FOR GREATER MEANING AT THE

SUPERMARKET OF RELIGION!

I WAS BORN METHODIST, BUT I'VE BECOME A HINDU... SO CAN YOU!
CUTE HOME ALTARS! · OBSCURE! DIFFERENT!

AFTERLIFES ARE FOR SAPS! I PREFER THE NEW TESTAMENT-FREE LIFESTYLE OF JUDAISM!
CAUTION: SUBJECT TO OCCASIONAL PERSECUTION.

I WAS TIRED OF GUILT AND EMOTION... SO I DITCHED THE POPE FOR PROTESTANTISM!
DULL! SAFE!
e-mail: tedrall@aol.com

IN SOUTH AMERICA, PRIESTS ARE GUN-TOTING REVOLUTIONARIES! ONLY CATHOLICISM OFFERS MARXIST CLERICS!
COOL RITUALS! A CLASSIC! · FEATURES "PENANCE"

AS AN ATHEIST, I DEVELOP MY OWN MORAL CODE!
TRENDY PEOPLE LIKE YOU MAKE ME SICK!
PICK ONE TODAY!
© 1995 CHRONICLE FEATURES

What to Say When Your Therapist Tells You You're Her Craziest Patient

by Bruce Smith

A year ago, I began to see the world with a new perspective. My lifelong interest in UFOs had reached a point where I believed not only were UFOs real, but extraterrestrials were here on Earth, and in fact, some had taken up permanent residence. What does that have to do with my psychotherapist? Well, I began to think she might be an alien.

Now some of you may think I'm crazy and are thanking God I'm seeking professional help. Others of you probably share my concern and are fervently hoping I terminate treatment right away in case she is an alien. I don't think too many people are blasé about this. There's not too much middle road on this issue. So let me defend myself, or at least explain why I thought my therapist might be an alien.

The prevailing view on aliens has been that they look like human beings but are cold to the touch. There are supposedly hundreds or thousands of these aliens roaming around our cities and streets, and the only way to identify them is with a physical touch. If they feel clammy cold, it's a good bet they're a visitor from very far away. In addition, I've come to learn, these aliens are here to study us, particularly our emotions, since back home on their Planet X they don't have any. They can't feel love, compassion or fear. Yeah, a tough life, I agree, but I began to realize that if I was an alien and here on earth to study emotions, the best way to do that would be as a psychotherapist. I know in my sessions there are emotions splashing all over the place. I cry in most sessions or sob so hard I can't breathe or talk, probably, twice a month. My psychotherapy would be a motherlode of emotion to study.

Plus if aliens are cold-blooded, and they

Callahan

"I dreamt I had a harem, but they all wanted to talk about the relationship."

Distributed by
Levin Represents

didn't want to be touched and detected, the best way to exist around here secretly would be as a psychotherapist from the analytical school of thought that requires the therapist to refrain from all physical touching.

As it turns out my therapist is from the no-touch school of psychotherapy. No hugging, handshakes, or pats-on-the-back. Nada! Most of the time that's okay, because my sexual fantasies or fears of intimacy are screaming all over the place, and if my therapist were to start getting touchy-feely with me, I'd really get anxious. But there are times I'd like a little normal human contact. Like, how about a Holiday Handshake at Christmas? How about a soft, reassuring pat-on-the-back after I've spent 45 minutes sobbing my eyes out over a girlfriend who's left me and I feel like no one in the world loves me. After all, I've been seeing this therapist for 3 years, and in a very unique way she's my best friend. Of course, she would say her job is to help me find my own friends, with whom I can share my feelings as well as I do with her, but who would also be able to be as affectionate with me as I wish? Yeah, blah, blah, blah...but to find such friends is a lot tougher than it sounds.

This anxiety about my therapist being an alien built to a point where I had to tell her. I don't always tell my therapist everything. I'm not that crazy. But when the pressure builds to such a point that I can't tolerate the squirming any longer, I blurt out whatever I have to. I was feeling scared. Suppose she was an alien and I had found her out? What would she do? Beam me up to her mother ship? Or worse, beam herself up and leave me all alone to face my life and this terrible truth?

My therapist was very surprised when I told her I thought she might be an alien. At first she thought I meant an illegal alien, like a Mexican fruit-picker.

"No, honey," I said, "UFO-type alien," teasing a bit. I knew I had gotten to her.

"What?" she replied softly. Intuitively I knew we were about to step into uncharted intra-psychic territory. Boldly I entered. I explained my understanding about the UFO invasion and the current state of things in the world. I was about to expand on a point of detail when she held up her hand, motioning me to stop.

"Let me get this straight. You really think I may be an alien from outer space, that I'm not really a human being?" she asked.

"Yes," I replied. And waited. Neither of us spoke for a long moment. Finally she leaned forward in her seat and rubbed her forehead, then looked at me sideways.

"That is the craziest thing I have ever heard," she stated.

"Ahah!" I laughed. I felt a certain joy at reaching a spot in the Psychiatric Hall of Fame for uttering a "craziest thing." I also felt relieved that she wasn't an alien. Not that I knew for sure, since she still hadn't touched me, but somehow my inner knowingness told me she was a human being. No alien, I figured, could fake looking as upset as my therapist now appeared.

I told my therapist I enjoyed being her "craziest patient," a title I felt I naturally deserved since I had uttered the "craziest thing." I bathed in a glow of feeling special. On the other hand, my therapist continued to look troubled, her face said silently, "Mister, you're a real sick puppy."

Then she asked, "Do you think we ought to discuss medication?"

"Hell, no," I replied, "I want to keep a clear head for this. Why don't I shake your hand and I'll see for myself whether you're alien clammy-cold, or human warm?"

"I don't think that would be a good idea," she said, with such finality in her voice that I was wholly intimidated. Why would such a simple test be unadvisable? Was she unwilling to jeopardize my three years of psychotherapy by letting me test the foibles of her body chemistry? Or was she simply afraid of me getting too close? Was she afraid that, despite her Ph.D. and post-doctoral training, I might be contagious? I never found out.

After a long silence, I decided I'd better cheer her up and change the subject. So I spent the remainder of my "UFO" session blithely talking about my sexual impotency, skin rashes, and reminiscences of the horrors of Catholic school. My therapist looked relieved and restored when I finally left that session.

We never discussed the incident again. Six months later I terminated treatment because I was moving out-of-state. After I handed her my final payment check, I stood and walked to the door. At the moment I reached for the doorknob, she said, "Wait a second."

I turned back toward her and saw her outstretched hand. She was offering me a handshake. After three years and more than 300 therapy sessions, I was about to have my first physical contact with my therapist. I reached for her hand, and grasped it.

It was the clammiest-cold hand I have ever touched.

My Cockroach Diary

by Sparrow

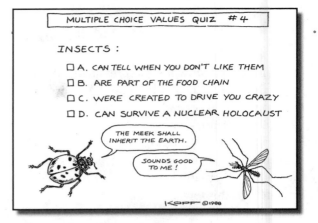

December 7

The cockroaches in this apartment have gone beyond all rational number – they have reached an irrational number. And they no longer wait until midnight to come out; they swarm after dark, at five. Ever since our visit to Russia in 1990, they've been increasing, and now they outnumber us four thousand to one.

Oh no, I just found one in the salt shaker! I helped it escape, using one of the baby's spoons.

December 8

This morning, three more cockroaches were in the salt shaker, but I couldn't find the baby's spoon. I used a larger spoon, which they refused to climb on. It was sad to see them struggling through the killing salt, dreaming of escape, but avoiding the instrument of salvation.

This must be how Christians see the world, I thought.

December 9

My wife woke up with a cockroach in her ear.

"It feels really strange. It's moving around," she said. She tried to take it out with a tissue wrapped around a chopstick.

"Let it crawl out," I told her. "If you kill it, it'll get stuck in there."

She stopped digging, and fifteen minutes later the bug did crawl out – a cute baby roach.

Now Violet is cleaning out the insect den under the sink. "Sorry, cockroaches. It's just not working out between us," she explains as she wipes away their nests.

"It smells of cockroach shit down here," she says to me.

I never knew cockroach shit had a smell.

December 10

Last night went well. There were fewer roaches than I have seen for months – as few as thirty-three.

But tonight we went to our neighbor's house to watch a video, and when we returned there were thousands again.

It's like trying to destroy the Mafia. You can arrest them, but you can't break their organization. These cockroaches have been at it for generations – it's all they know. The kids go into it because their fathers do it.

December 13

Until now we haven't killed the roaches. We've employed preventive methods; doing the dishes right away, taking the garbage out daily. Then last night, while washing dishes, I noticed a roach crawling on the side of a cup. I made no effort to save him, and in a moment he had drowned. A certain hardness has crept into me, I realized.

When I bathe now, and notice three or four roach corpses in the tub – drowned as the water poured in – I feel a grim satisfaction.

I wonder, "Could I kill a man now?"

December 17

A cockroach has been trapped in the salt-shaker all day, and I've done nothing. I'm bored with liberating them over and over. He walks around while I pour salt out from under him. It's like having a tiny man living in your watch.

January 4

At our New Year's party, Norman announced, "I think you have a roach problem."

"Why do you say that?"

"Because I've seen several roaches walking

around next to the food. If roaches come out in the middle of a party, you have a problem."

"I've already killed six of them," added Violet's cousin Bill.

"I bet you don't kill them," Norman accused me. "You probably tell them to leave. I had a roommate like that in San Francisco. We lived above a carriage house in an alley, and we had a bad roach problem. He believed that if he told them to leave, they would go. He'd say to them, 'Roaches, please don't stay here. We don't really want you here.'"

"Did they listen to him?"

"Of course not. They got worse."

"So what did you do?"

"I called in the exterminator. He came three times, and then the roaches were gone."

Violet said, "But our friend Therese told the cockroaches to leave an apartment, and they left."

"Yeah," I told Norman. "Your friend probably wasn't spiritually evolved enough."

"Well, the roaches aren't listening to you either!" Norman said.

January 5

I forgot to tell Norman my favorite roach-killing story – the time a guy came to my door in Washington Heights and asked, "Do you want to be exterminated?"

January 16

It's unfortunate that we had our baby, Sylvia, in the middle of this cockroach war, because a baby's job is to eat one-eighteenth of a potato, then throw the rest on the floor for you to step on, and the whole time you're thinking, "She's feeding the damn roaches. She's in league with them."

January 19

Today as I drank some tea, I thought I saw a fleck floating in it. Is it a baby cockroach? I wondered. I looked more closely, and it seemed benign.

After I finished the tea, I thought, perhaps it was a roach. Maybe I eat cockroaches every day. They run out of a pot of millet sometimes. But does every one run out?

How many roaches a day do I eat?

January 21

My mother came over to babysit and said, "I'm having such a roach problem. I got a small garbage can with a tight lid, but it doesn't help. I just can't cope with my roaches anymore!"

This reassured me. Perhaps roach problems are hereditary.

January 22

Today I was working on my novel, and a bug walked out on the desk in front of me. I looked down in anger, then saw it wasn't a roach. It was a gray, horned creature, like a miniature toad. I almost kissed it, out of gratitude.

January 26

"Lately when I open the cupboard doors," my wife said, "a cockroach usually falls on my head. It's really obnoxious."

"I've noticed it, too. Are they leaning on the doors more than they used to?"

March 10

Violet woke up with another cockroach in her ear. "It's really loud," she said. "It's walking on my eardrum."

"Did you try to take it out?"

"No. Now it's stopped moving," she said.

"Can you look in my ear?" (We bought a speculum to check the baby's ears for infections.)

"OK," I said, but we both forgot.

March 12

I remembered to look in Violet's ear. Inside was a small dead cockroach, curled on its back.

It's strange to see a dead roach in your wife's ear. A little scene in there – like looking at a Viewmaster.

Violet tried to extract it, failed, and agreed to see a doctor.

March 15

Violet is procrastinating about going to the doctor. Meanwhile, as I was meditating tonight at 1:00 A.M., I felt a cockroach in my ear. It crawled deeper and deeper, perhaps into my brain. (Does the brain connect with the ear? I wasn't sure.)

I continued meditating and found myself speaking mentally to the insect: "Turn around! That's a good roach!"

Not that I believe in talking to roaches.

When I finished my meditation, I asked Violet, "Are you awake?"

"Give me the can Bob, don't be foolish, don't make me use this!"

"Yes."

"Can you look in my ear?"

She looked in my ear. "It's a hair," she said. "It's touching your eardrum."

Now I'm in the Bellevue emergency room, waiting for a doctor. It's 2:30 A.M. I was hoping there would be no line on a quiet winter night, but I forgot that the homeless come here to stay warm. So thirty-eight men and one woman are waiting with me as an infomercial plays on the television above us: "I made a fortune investing in real estate. So can you."

Once in a while the police pass through with a young, handcuffed criminal. They walk right in without waiting.

After two hours and forty-five minutes, I got to see a doctor. "What seems to be the problem?" he asked.

"I have a hair in my ear," I said.

"Um humm." He got a speculum and looked inside.

"You're right. There's something in there. It looks like a hair." (But to another doctor, he muttered, "It isn't a hair.")

"It might be a cockroach," I volunteered. "My wife has a cockroach in her ear."

"Why doesn't she take it out?" the doctor asked.

"She's been busy."

The doctor looked in my ear again. "It looks like a cockroach," he said. "I saw it moving."

"Really?" I said. I felt a cockroach in my ear. I felt it move.

Another doctor came to look. "I don't see anything," he said.

My doctor put a long Q-tip in my ear. He pulled it out. Nothing was on it. He handed me the Q-tip. "You try it. You can feel it in there."

I put it in. The two doctors watched. I pulled out the Q-tip. A tiny cat hair was on the end.

The doctors looked disappointed.

One took the Q-tip with the hair. "Can I throw it out, or do you want to keep it as a souvenir?"

"Throw it out," I said.

They gave me a bill for $295, and I left.

March 17

I am going to begin killing the roaches with my own two hands.

March 22

I killed my first roach. It was a baby that crawled out of my novel when I opened it.

It took me five tries to kill it. They have very hard skins. I admitted to Violet that I'm killing the roaches.

"So am I," she said sheepishly, "though I feel guilty about it."

"I wouldn't mind them if they didn't crawl into our ears."

"Well, they haven't crawled into your ears."

"We don't know. Maybe they crawl in and crawl out."

March 23

Soon after I killed the first roach, the others began running faster when I approached. They must have a sophisticated communication network between the living and the dead.

Since then, I've cataloged a number of roach species: a dark-colored one, a squat one, a long, thin one.

Strange I'd never noticed them before. You don't really see something until you kill it.

March 26

I came home late from work and Violet said, "The house is clean, isn't it?"

"Yes, it is!"

"I killed a lot of cockroaches," she said.

"Oh, yeah? How did it feel?"

"Terrible. When I killed a little one, I would think, 'That's someone's baby.'"

"Yes, but I doubt the mothers love their babies as much as you do."

"And when I killed a big one, I thought, 'Maybe it's a pregnant one,' and felt horribly guilty."

We hugged.

May 28

I began killing roaches again at the sink out of frustration. But in the middle of my death spree, I remembered Darwin's Theory of Natural Selection.

"Wait a second," I told my wife. "If I kill all the slow ones, only the fast ones will survive, and we'll have the fastest roaches on earth!"

June 17

Violet, Sylvia, and I took a trip to Israel. I was struck by the utter buglessness of our Tel Aviv hotel, though it was in a hot, Middle Eastern country.

A great deal of poison must be responsible, I thought with a shudder.

Also, the room felt lonely – there was no one in it but us.

A Little Misunderstanding

by Marcia Frigaard Steil

FLY CASTING

WE'LL CALL YOU

NICOLOFF

As Corrine Bender lifted the garage door, she became aware of the odor. Warily she stepped into the darkened garage, but it was apparently empty. She stopped near a pile of newspapers she was saving for the recycling center. At her feet was a scattering of cigarette butts. The garage smelled of the smoke.

"That does it," she exclaimed. Corrine marched inside and called the police.

For three weeks it had been evident that neighborhood teenagers had been using her garage and backyard as a meeting place while she was gone. It had started shortly after she took a part-time job at the bank. Summer vacation had left a few of the neighborhood children with nothing to do.

"They have done no damage," she told the desk sergeant on the phone, "but they are trespassing and I am concerned about a fire; today the cigarette butts were dangerously close to some papers in the garage." At least they were regular cigarettes.

"Technically, they are breaking the law," the sergeant replied. "Since you say you've already tried to talk to them and had no success, I'll send someone out."

Corrine sighed as she hung up. She was not totally comfortable with her decision. There had to be a better way to deal with the situation.

Morton Deebs was also uncomfortable. When you drove a van that carried a four-foot plastic cockroach on the roof, people stared. Not that he blamed them. Would he have been less uncomfortable had the cockroach not been positioned upon its back, its incompliant legs reaching unceremoniously for the sky? It was really quite undignified, thought Morton, as he pulled into a quiet cul de sac. Had he owned Conrad Exterminators, the roach would be the first thing to go. He sensed that clients did not care to advertise to the neighbors that they had a need for his services, and the cockroach certainly announced quite plainly the purpose of his visit.

Morton Deebs parked on the corner, back away from the houses. The order sheet indicated that 709 Aspen Avenue was in need of roach ridding. 709 Aspen was a tidy white cottage with green shutters. Morton approved; he was, himself, a tidy man.

The order indicated that he should arrive no sooner than two o'clock and it was only one. He left the equipment in the van. No use hauling it to the door if no one was home. He walked past the neatly trimmed hedge and rang the bell. The lady of the house answered.

"Oh! Come right in," said the pleasant looking woman who answered the door. "Thank you so much for coming."

"How do you do? I'm Morton Deebs. May I have your name? It seems to have been left off my order sheet."

"Of course. I'm Corrine Bender."

Morton copied the name carefully. "I understand you have a problem."

"I do, indeed." Corrine ushered the man into the living room. "I want you to understand that they haven't done any real damage yet..."

"But you wouldn't want to wait until that happens, would you? Better to deal with it now."

"Of course. And they deserve to be punished," stated Corrine firmly.

"Punished?"

"That's not my only motive for calling you here, though. I'm doing this for their own good, even though they won't realize it." Corrine was still concerned about neighborhood reaction to her call to the police.

"You know, I didn't just panic and call you the first thing. I tried to deal with the problem directly myself."

"Well, Mrs. Bender, that's most commendable. But most people find this sort of situation requires the services of a professional."

Morton Deebs had been in pest control for three years. In that time, he had heard of people stepping on cockroaches, spraying them with aerosol canisters, poisoning them, trapping them in sticky little boxes, and moving away from them by selling the family home. Morton Deebs had never met anyone who had tried talking to them.

"I tried," continued Corrine, "to be pleasant to them, to reason with them."

"How... how did they react?" stammered Morton Deebs.

"It had no effect whatsoever. They continued pestering me."

At this point, Morton felt he had two choices. He could excuse himself and leave. Or he could do his job as quickly as possible. And leave. The main thing was to leave, because this lady was a little strange. But Morton, being a tidy man, did not like leaving things undone. He stood resolutely.

"Now that I'm here, you won't have to worry about a thing. I'll see that they never bother you again. Tell me where you've noticed them."

"In the back yard and the garage," replied Corrine. She liked the no-nonsense attitude of this man. He would take care of everything.

"Okay, but I'm going to check out the house as well."

"Oh," Corrine's hand flew to her mouth. "I'm sure they haven't come into the house."

But Corrine glanced around. The thought made her quite uncomfortable.

"You would be surprised and shocked, Mrs. Bender, at the places they find to hide." With the authority of a man who is going to get the job done, Morton headed for the kitchen.

"Wait!" Corrine for a moment was concerned about his manner. She wanted the problem dealt with, but would he be tactful or would he alienate her from the neighbors?

"Perhaps it's not necessary for you to see them today. Actually, I was hoping that seeing your car parked out front would throw a scare into them."

Morton Deebs stopped so suddenly that Mrs. Bender nearly collided with him. As it was, he had to step back to avoid standing nose to nose with the woman. He had never before met anyone who was crazy. A more curious man would have paused and questioned. A witty man would have quipped, "Perhaps I could play a flute and we could lead them all out to the front yard for a good look."

But Morton was neither a curious man nor a witty one. The lady had bats in her belfry, but she also had cockroaches in her garage — and probably in her kitchen too, if Morton Deebs knew his cockroaches.

"I'll just take a moment," said Morton as he turned and kneeled on the kitchen floor and opened the doors of the cupboard under

"Ah, ha!!"

Corrine's sink. He ducked his head in, pulled out a tiny flashlight, and made a quick search.

Had Mr. Deebs been looking, he would have see Corrine's jaw drop noticeably, her eyes widen, and her hand fly to her breast.

Of course, Morton did not see these things, his head being under the sink in a cupboard. And it was just this circumstance which caused Corrine's reaction. She had never had a policeman in her cupboard before. She was not expecting one to be there today. Corrine did not like the unexpected. She turned to look at the clock. Her husband, Frank, would not be home for hours. Did one scream under such circumstances? Corrine did not have time to decide what the appropriate behavior was.

"Now," announced Morton Deebs, "I'll check your attic."

"My attic?"

"The attic," lectured Morton, as he strode down the hall, "is a favorite hiding place. They like to hide between the walls, too."

"Wait, I assure you, it is not necessary to search my attic."

Corrine was successful in steering Morton Deebs back to the living room. Morton was losing patience.

"Mrs. Bender, if I am not to be permitted to handle this situation in my own way, then perhaps I'd better leave."

"I think I need to hear more about your methods before we take this any further," said Corrine Bender firmly. This man was not behaving in an appropriate manner at all. And, to her relief, he had just offered to leave, which meant he did not intend to harm her.

"What would you like to know?" asked Morton Deebs.

"I can tell you where they are. What I want to know is what do you intend to do with them when you find them?" asked Corrine Bender.

Morton Deebs took a breath. As if speaking to a very slow child, he replied, "I am going to kill them."

The blood drained from Corrine Bender's face. Her heart pounded loudly in her chest — so loudly that her hands flew to cover her ears. Her eyes snapped open in horror. Get the man

out and then get help. But be careful. Don't alarm him. She brought her hands down and smoothed her dress.

"I thought, perhaps, just a warning this time."

"You've already tried that, Mrs. Bender," Morton carefully replied.

"But coming from you, a warning would mean so much more to them."

Morton Deebs could not picture himself talking to cockroaches, even to appease a customer. Such behavior did not reflect the dignity with which Morton credited himself.

"Mrs. Bender, I've been in this business for several years and I've never met one you could reason with."

Morton Deebs headed for the door. He had never lost a customer before, and he wasn't sure how he was going to explain this to Mr. Conrad.

"I'm sorry to have wasted your time, but I can't let you hurt them," said Corrine as she walked him to the door.

"It has been," replied Morton Deebs, "a most interesting experience."

As he walked down the sidewalk, he pulled the order sheet from his pocket. He would have to figure out what he was going to write on it; he certainly had not completed the job.

"Oh, dear," whispered Morton Deebs to himself. Instead of visiting 709 Aspen Lane, he had knocked on the wrong door and visited 706 instead. He checked his watch. It was 1:30. He still had time to make the appointment.

As Morton Deebs was ringing the bell at 709, Corrine Bender was standing openmouthed in her front yard staring at an absurd van parked a short distance away. Atop the vehicle was a very large, dead, four-foot cockroach. There was no patrol car in sight.

Moments later, however, one pulled up at 706 Aspen Lane. The neighborhood seemed, to the police officer in the driver's seat, to be pleasant and quiet, except for the woman sitting on the lawn, laughing uncontrollably as tears rolled down her face. She was, obviously, hysterical.

Science

Better Than Sex: Confessions Of a Political Junkie

by Hunter S. Thompson

John F. Kennedy, who seized the White House from Richard Nixon in a frenzied campaign that turned a whole generation of young Americans into political junkies, got shot in the head for his efforts, murdered in Dallas by some hapless geek named Oswald who worked for either Castro, the mob, Jimmy Hoffa, the CIA, his dominatrix landlady or the odious, degenerate FBI chief J. Edgar Hoover. The list is long and crazy — maybe Marilyn Monroe's first husband fired those shots from the Grassy Knoll. Who knows? A whole generation of American journalists is still embarrassed by their failure to answer that question.

JFK's ghost will haunt the corridors of power in America for as long as the grass is green and the rivers run to the sea... take my word for it, Bubba. I have heard his footsteps for 30 years and I still feel guilty about not being able to explain the biggest news story of my lifetime to my son.

At one point, not long ago, I went to the desperate length of confessing to the murder myself. We were finishing breakfast in a patio restaurant on a bright Sunday morning in Boulder. It was a stylish place near the campus, where decent people could meet after pretending they had just come from church and get fashionably drunk on mimosas and white wine. The tables were separated by ferns and potted palms. Bright orange impatiens flowers drooped from hanging urns.

Even I can't explain why I said what I did. I had been up all night with my old friend Allen Ginsberg, the poet, and we had both slid into the abyss of whiskey madness and full-bore substance abuse. It was wonderful, but it left me a little giddy by the time noon rolled around.

"Son," I said, "I'm sorry to ruin your breakfast, but I think the time has finally come to tell you the truth about who shot John Kennedy."

He nodded but said nothing. I tried to keep my voice low, but emotion made it difficult.

"It was me," I said. "I am the one who shot Jack Kennedy."

"What?" he said, glancing quickly over his shoulder to see if others were listening. Which they were. The mention of Kennedy's name will always turn a few heads, anywhere in the world — and God only knows what a tenured professor of American political history might feel upon hearing some grizzled thug in a fern bar confess to his own son that he was the one who murdered John F. Kennedy. It is one of those lines that will not fall on deaf ears.

My son leaned forward and stared into my eyes as I explained the raw details and my reasons for killing the President in cold blood, many years ago. I spoke about ballistics and treachery and my "secret work for the government" in Brazil, when he thought I was in the Peace Corps in the sixties.

"I gave up killing about the time you were

born," I said. "But I could never tell you about it, until now."

He nodded solemnly for a moment, then laughed at me and called for some tea. "Don't worry, Dad," he said.

"Good boy," I said. "Now we can finally be honest with each other. I feel naked and clean for the first time in 30 years."

"Not me," he said. "Now I'll have to turn you in."

"What?" I shouted. "You treacherous little bastard!" Many heads turned to stare at us. It was a weird moment for them. The man who killed Kennedy had just confessed publicly to his son, and now they were cursing each other. Ye gods, what next?

What indeed? How warped can it be for a child born into the sixties to finally be told that his father was the hired shootist who killed Kennedy? Do you call 911? Call a priest? Or act like a cockroach and say nothing?

No wonder the poor bastards from Generation X have lost their sense of humor about politics. Some things are not funny to the doomed, especially when they've just elected a President with no sense of humor at all. The joke is over when even victory is a downhill run into hardship, disappointment and a queasy sense of betrayal. If you can laugh in the face of these things, you are probably ready for a staff job with a serious presidential candidate. The humor of the campaign trail is relentlessly cruel and brutal. If you think you like jokes, try hanging around the cooler after

midnight with hired killers like James Carville or the late Lee Atwater, whose death by cancer in 1991 was a fatal loss to the Bush re-election effort. Atwater could say, without rancor, that he wanted to castrate Michael Dukakis and dump him on the Boston Common with his nuts stuffed down his throat. Atwater said a lot of things that made people cringe, but he usually smiled when he said them, and people tried to laugh.

It was Deep Background stuff, they figured; of course he didn't mean it. Hell, in some states you could go to prison for making threats like that. Felony Menacing, two years minimum; Conspiracy to Commit Murder and/or Felony Assault with Intent to Commit Great Bodily Harm, minimum 50 years in Arkansas and Texas; also Kidnapping (death), Rape, Sodomy, Malicious Disfigurement, Treason, Perjury, Gross Sexual Imposition and Aggravated Conspiracy to commit all of the above (600 years, minimum). And all of this without anybody ever doing anything. Ho, ho. How's that for the wheels of justice, Bubba? Six hundred fifty-two years, just for downing a few ginbucks at lunch and trading jokes among warriors...

Richard Nixon was not a crook. Ho, ho.

George Bush was innocent. Ho, ho.

Ed Rollins bribed every Negro preacher in New Jersey to hold down the black vote for the Governor in '93. Hee-haw.

That is the kind of humor that campaign junkies admire and will tell to their children —

for the same perverse reasons that make me confess to my son, over breakfast, that I blew John Kennedy's head off in Dallas.

You have to be very mean to get a laugh on the campaign trail. There is no such thing as paranoia.

Not everybody will get a laugh out of these things, but if you want to get elected, it is better to be Mean than to be Funny.

Cruel jokes are a big part of life in any environment where speed freaks, work addicts and obsessive-compulsive political junkies are ripped to the tits day and night for thirteen straight months on their own adrenaline. Swollen more and more each day with the kind of hubris that comes when you try to cross Innocence and Ambition all at once and you start seeing yourself on the front page of the *New York Times* in a photo with the next president getting off a jet plane in Texas or Boston or Washington, surrounded by a gang of hard-eye U.S. Secret Service agents escorting you through the cheering crowd.

It's a rush that a lot of people will tell you is higher than any drug they've ever tried or even heard about, and maybe better than sex...which is a weird theory and often raises unsettling personal questions, but it is a theory nonetheless, and on some days I've even believed it myself.

But not really, and days like that are so rare that I usually can't even remember them, but when I do, it is like a nail in my eye. The pain goes away, but the wound stays forever. The scar never quite heals over – and whenever it

seems like it's going to, I pick at it. I have some scars that go back 33 years, and I still remember how they happened, just like it was yesterday.

Not everybody is comfortable with the idea that politics is a guilty addiction. But it is. They are addicts, and they are guilty and they do lie and cheat and steal – like all junkies. And when they get in a frenzy, they will sacrifice anything and anybody to feed their cruel and stupid habit, and there is no cure for it. That is addictive thinking. That is politics – especially in presidential campaigns. That is when the addicts seize the high ground. They care about nothing else. They are salmon, and they must spawn. They are addicts, and so am I. The fish hear their music and I hear mine. Politics is like the Guinea Worm. It sneaks into your body and grows like a cyst from within – until finally it gets so big and strong that it bursts straight through the skin, a horrible red worm with a head like a tiny cobra, snapping around in the air as it struggles to breathe.

This is true. There are pictures of it happening, in the *Encyclopedia Britannica*. The Guinea Worm is real...and so is politics, for that matter. The only difference is that you can get rid of the worm by gripping its head and wrapping its body around a stick, then pulling it very slowly out of your flesh, like a bird pulls an earth worm out of the ground.

Getting rid of a political addiction is not so easy. The worm is smaller and tends to migrate upward, to the skull, where it feeds and thrives on the tissue. It is undetectable, in the early stage, usually diagnosed by a common "brain fluke" – which is also incurable – and by the time it gets powerful enough to bore its way through a soft spot in the skull, not even witch doctors will touch it.

The Guinea Worm problem is confined mainly to equatorial Africa, thank God. We are not ready for it in this country. A declining standard of living is one thing, but getting used to the notion that any lesion on your leg might be the first sign of a worm about to erupt is still unacceptable to the normal American. Even a single (confirmed) case of Guinea Worm in Washington would be taken as an omen and doom Bill Clinton's presidency. An epidemic would finish the Democratic party and put Pat Buchanan in the White House for 20 years.

That is a horrible scenario, Bubba, and it probably won't happen. We have enough trouble in Washington without the goddamn Guinea Worm – although many presidents have suffered from worse things, but these were always kept secret from the public.

That is the job of the Secret Service, and they are good at it. "Degenerates are our specialty," one agent joked. "We cover up things every day of the week that would embarrass the Marquis de Sade."

Sex and the Single Chevy

by Penny Wallace

"I don't know what it is about you, Monica, but I've loved you from the moment I saw you."

You want to meet a man? I'll tell you how to meet a man. Put an ad in your local paper for a 1977 Chevy Malibu Classic. I can't guarantee he'll show up in a three-piece suit with the *Wall Street Journal* under his arm, but I can guarantee you'll have more men calling than you could date through the millennium.

If you count all the calls, including the hang-ups after my machine announced the car had been sold, I'd estimate conservatively that I got about 150. My personals ad drew only 62, and those guys were so damn nervous. Not the Chevy guys. They're anxious all right, but not about me. These guys are for real, in their element. They're big-game hunters, and there's something thrilling about a man with a mission.

I promised the car to the first guy who showed up, Mike, but succumbed to pressure to actually sell to the second who arrived, breathless, just after Mike left. He simply had to have that car.

The first guy came equipped with a wife and kid. The second was a repo man from Brooklyn...not exactly my type.

The question, in retrospect, is how does a girl get to meet all these guys if she gives up the car to the first one who comes begging? And trust me, they will be begging – body rot or no body rot. If I hadn't put a dent in the front fender I would have had guys lying prostrate at my feet. I knew it was a desirable car, but I never suspected it would hold such fascination for so many.

I was selling it for Mom, the quintessential little old lady who'd only used it to go to the kosher meat market on Fridays. The ad was straightforward and I'm quite sure the phrase "34,000 original miles/original owner" didn't detract in the least. My phone began ringing the moment the newspaper hit the streets.

And closing the deal didn't slow down the other 148 desperados clamoring for the precious hunk of metal. The phone kept ringing.

At first I was annoyed by the volume of calls. I canceled the ad to ward off laryngitis. But the phone kept ringing. After the first 35, I let my machine pick up. "Hi," it said, "this is Penny. If you're calling about the Chevy, sorry, it's been sold; if you're calling about me, leave a message."

Some time late in the afternoon on the second day I realized my shortsightedness. I arrived home, checked my answering machine and found a chatty message left in the style of an avuncular Telly Savalas: "Hey listen, don't be sorry it's sold. You sold the car, you're happy, you got your money, right?

Don't worry about it! I'll get another car. Have a nice day." I loved this guy – friendly, easy-going, good philosophy. I was sure that if I'd been home, at the very least we would have had a great conversation. And who knows what might have followed...

The next message was pleasant enough, but you could tell the guy was moderately depressive, inarticulate, defeatist; definitely not dating material: "Yeah, uh, hello, Penny, oh, yes, I was calling about the Chevy, but, uh, sorry to hear it was sold, uh, have a nice day." At least he, too, wanted me to have a nice day, and he got points for using my name, but the overall tone was uninspiring. The next call made up for it though: "Ah, too bad about the Chevy but you sound cute. Well, I'm married. Take care."

I didn't need an advanced degree to appreciate the potential gold mine lying in wait just at the other end of my phone line. I abandoned the answering machine in favor of some old-fashioned direct contact. And the calls kept coming.

I varied my phone technique depending on the tone of the guy's voice. There were a few women who called, but only because their husbands didn't have phones at work. We talked about the Chevy, me and the guys, mutually extolling its virtues. I'd admit that I'd

taken a deposit, but that "well, you know how it is these days with the economy; you can't consider it a done deal till all the money's changed hands." It was important to keep their hopes up.

And, just in case the deal fell through, I got their names. I got their phone numbers, their addresses. Their marital status. I put little coded symbols beside their names indicating my interest level depending on how well the conversation went.

Now that I've given the matter a bit more thought, I realize there's way more potential in this concept than I'd originally suspected. The truth is, I see no reason why one would need to actually own a '77 Chevy Malibu Classic to begin with. As a matter of fact, I understand the '62 Porsche Speedster is a very desirable car...

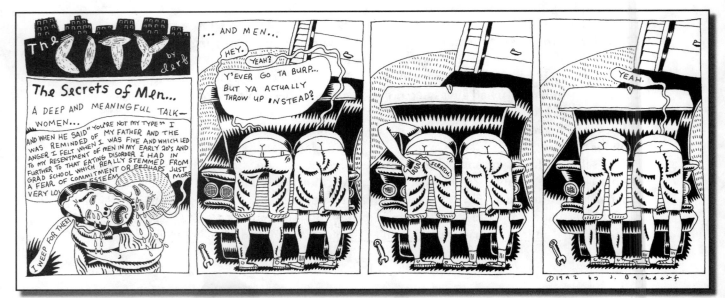

Work

"At last we've reached a consensus!
This meeting is boring!"

"PLEASE DON'T BE ANGRY OR I'LL HAVE TO TRANSFER YOU AGAIN."

WE VALUE EMPLOYEE SUGGESTIONS

Whose job can be eliminated next?

Receive a crisp $50 bill!

The problems with whale farming

Plankton, plankton, plankton, twenty-four stinking hours a day...

"It's bullshit, yes, but a new form of bullshit."

Christopher Zell

"Now what the fuck are we going to do?"

HI HO, HI HO,...IT'S OFF TO WORK WE GO!

DEPRESSED?.. TAKE SOME PILLS!

BOO-HOO. HOO

ANGRY?.. TAKE SOME PILLS!

CONFUSED?.. TAKE SOME PILLS!

WHAT DOSE IT ALL MEAN?

FEELING BETTER?.. GOOD! NOW GO BACK TO WORK!!

I'M CURED

Sidewalk Bubblegum ©1995 Clay Butler

GOFF

"AND THAT'S WHY I NEED A VACATION."

"You're hired, Hoskins. I'll have my secretary blow up a desk and chair immediately."

Susan has solved the problem of balancing work and home by eliminating her personal life altogether.

"And this is the secret of how our company stays competitive today: We grow all our own food!"

"Gentlemen, I don't have time for this. I'm running on a very tight asshole!"

City finds employment for rollerblader.

"I HATE OFFICE POLITICS... IT JUST SO HAPPENS THAT I ENJOY MOWING THE BOSS'S LAWN."

Corporate Bob

A Tele-commuter's casual day

He had done all the big adult stuff.
Now, maybe they would leave him alone.

Red the Rat Man

by Bailey White

One night I heard scampering and thumping in the walls. My first impulse was call Red the Rat Man. But Red the Rat Man has been dead for fifteen years. Besides, I remembered, toward the end he wouldn't kill rats anyway.

In his early days, Red the Rat Man was a wizard exterminator. He knew and understood rats. "You got to know the mind of a rat," Red the Rat Man would say, tapping his own head. "The mind of a rat."

Then he would disappear under the house, dragging a jar of peanut butter, a roll of wire, and traps of all sizes. He didn't believe in rat poison. "The rats eat that poison, then they crawl into your walls and die. Stink up the place. Besides," he would add, turning away, "it's a suffering death, with poison. Traps kill 'em clean."

There would be some scuffling noises under the house, and some snaps and clicks, and after a while he would crawl out, brush off his knees, and drive off in his rickety old pickup truck with "Red the Rat Man" stenciled on the door. For five years or more we would not see or hear a rat in our house.

Of all rats, Red the Rat Man admired pack rats the most. "They are the most intelligent of rats," he would tell us. When he found a pack rat nest under the house, he would make us all crawl under there with him to see it. It would be lined with soft fur and decorated with nandina berries. There would be shiny things glinting in the straw, and bright bits of fabric. "Red is the favorite color of the pack rat," Red the Rat Man would say.

On the rare occasions when he managed to catch a pack rat in a trap, he would make us all gather round. He would reverently lay the dead rat on its back and stroke its white belly.

IF KITTENS WERE AS BIG AS HOUSES, THEY WOULD PLAY WITH US UNTIL WE DIE

"See here," he would say, parting the rat's front legs, "two little titties, right on her chest." And sure enough, there they would be, two pink nipples. "Onliest animals that have that is people, elephants, and pack rats." Red the Rat Man would hold the dead rat in his two hands and shake his head. "A noble rat," he would say. "The prince of rats."

There's something endearing about a man who loves rats, and women kept marrying Red the Rat Man. Each one thought she could cure him of his terrible alcoholism and turn him around. But as is so often the way, the thing that is the sweetest in the beginning is the very thing that rankles in the end; the wives were neglected and ignored while the rats held sway, and one after the other they left Red the Rat Man to his rats and his gin.

Years passed. Red the Rat Man's back became stooped, his hands shook, and his eyes were bleary. More and more often rats would reappear just days after his visit. "That Red the Rat Man's lost his touch," people began to say.

Then the new exterminator moved into our area. He wore a white uniform and carried a spray can of poison with a long wand. Pretty soon he began spreading stories about Red the Rat Man.

Everywhere Red the Rat Man had been, the new exterminator said, he was finding the same thing. All the traps were baited, but none of them was set. And beside every trap was a handful of strange-looking nuggets. "I thought they were rat poison at first," the new exterminator said. "But when I got out in the light, I saw that they were nothing but dried lima beans. Dried lima beans painted bright red with enamel paint.

"It was a great gift he had, Red the Rat Man, as an exterminator," the new rat man said. "Too bad he let his emotions get in the way."

Now the rats were back at my house, and they were driving me crazy. I suspected they were pack rats because they were too smart to get themselves caught in the traps I set for them. And we seemed to share the same taste in fashion. They stole my beaten silver bracelet from Spain, my scarab ring, and my silk twill scarf from the Metropolitan Museum of Art. They stole my narcissus bulbs that I had been so carefully forcing to bloom in January. They stole my shiny multicolored rocks I had brought all the way from the Snake River in Idaho.

I lay in my bed and listened all night long to the rats rattling the rocks and rolling the bulbs around in the wall behind my bed. I wrapped the pillow around my head. "Damn your nobility, damn your two titties, damn your elegant taste," I ranted. I didn't get much sleep.

Finally, the night came when I couldn't stand it anymore. The moon was full and the rats were lively. They were playing ninepin with my narcissus bulbs. I hurled myself out of bed, charged out to the tool chest, and got a crowbar. I pried a batten off the wall behind my bed. From inside I heard scampering, then silence. I pulled a couple of nails and slid out a board. I shined my flashlight into the space.

There was a huge rat's nest. It was lined with soft fur and my fringed silk scarf. One crimson rose had been neatly excised from the scarf's design, and its red fibers were woven in with the fur. Strips of tinfoil glinted. My red and green and blue rocks with their veins of gold glowed in the light. There was my silver bracelet and my scarab ring. And my narcissus bulbs were artistically arranged in a kind of serpentine wall around the whole thing.

I put a finger into the nest. It was so soft I couldn't even tell I was touching anything. There was a baby rat. It was pink and its eyes weren't open. I parted its front legs and shined my light. Sure enough, two little titties.

Very gently, I pulled out the silver bracelet. I was careful not to disturb anything else. Then I slid the board back in place. I nailed the batten back on top. My bed is on casters, and I rolled it across the room. From that distance the noise wouldn't seem so loud. I crawled under the covers and closed my eyes. "For you, Red the Rat Man," I whispered.

I slept peacefully all night long. And in the morning when I went into the bathroom, there was a little pile of something. An offering. Seven dried lima beans, painted red.

1ˢᵀ NATIONAL RODENTS BANK

You Know You Don't Have a Life When...

by Ken Wickerham

YOU KNOW YOU DON'T HAVE A LIFE WHEN...

...you enter the Publishers Clearinghouse Sweepstakes.

...you have more than three remotes.

...you iron your underwear.

...you have no weeds in your lawn.

...you yell at the umpires at Little League games.

...you have a Star Trek uniform.

...you understand and enjoy weather maps.

...you call into radio talk shows.

...you go ballistic when the ice trays haven't been filled.

...you have dogs running around the house with bigger genitalia than you.

...everything in your living room is pointing toward the TV.

...your house has wheels and taillights.

...you walk behind an animal while carrying a little shovel and a turd in a bag.

...you discuss football strategy in the same tones as stock market analysts discuss the economy.

...you "boot up" your computer because it's fun to say.

...you wish people would be more in touch with your feelings.

...you invite your young relatives to "pull your finger."

...you holler "fore" as you drive by a golf course.

...you get into fist fights defending your brand of beer.

A Women's Weekend

by Maxine Wilkie

Every summer for the past five years, I've participated in a female ritual. Along with three old friends, I spend the weekend at a cabin on Lake Tahoe in California. This is a special group of women. Between us, there are two nurses, four advanced degrees, two Ph.D.s, one professor, one award-winning baker, and an epidemiologist. Two women have husbands, and three are divorced. One doesn't want children and two of us have infertility problems. We've had six pregnancies, two miscarriages, four sons and one daughter, so far. Altogether we've seen almost every continent and most new movies. One of us invariably has her period. We meet near San Francisco on Thursday afternoon, load the car with endless suitcases and unfinished needlework projects, and head for the hills.

This is supposed to be the kind of weekend that they make female-buddy movies about — dear old friends meeting year after year to give each other support and reassurance. Initially, we buy into that image too. Every year we foresee evenings in front of the fireplace after a vigorous afternoon walk in the woods, a glass of expensive white wine in hand, discussing what it means to be a woman of the nineties. We plan educational sight-seeing trips and gourmet meals. We make a list of current events that we should discuss.

But instead, the weekend always falls short of these lofty goals and ends up reflecting what we really are, and what we've always been — chocolate craving babes out to have a good time.

The major problem, I think, and what sends the weekend immediately downhill, is its location. The house is great — right on the lake with a large picture window displaying the grandeur of Lake Tahoe at our feet. But who cares? There's also a Safeway right across the street. With that Mecca of junk food and trashy magazines in such close proximity, who has time to soak in the view? We always drive in about 4 P.M., and by 4:05 someone has pencil in hand and is making a list for the store. "OK," says Ann, the one who maintains a facade of class and meaning the longest, "We should have lots of fruit, and what about bran muffins for breakfast?" "Right," answers

IN THE LAND OF WOMEN WHO PEEK UNDER MEN'S PANTS

Becky, rolling her eyes at Ann's optimism, "and don't forget the red licorice." "Be sure to get the large size chocolate chips," adds Kathy. "Maybe this year someone will actually cook those cookies before we eat all the dough." No one need mention the M&Ms since the first person to the grocery store is expected, under threat of endless ridicule, to bring back the largest sized bags of plain and peanut. Everyone plops on the sofa like beached whales until the M&Ms are installed in their traditional star-shaped blue bowl and we can muster enough energy to unload the car.

The house quickly begins to look like a girls' camp where the campers are in charge, or maybe a flu ward where the patients are faking it just to stay home from school. Becky soon takes off her perfectly matched sweater, skirt and earring ensemble and throws on her bathrobe, and she doesn't peel it off for three days. Kathy wipes off her makeup and puts on sweats, only to emerge as her "street self" the morning we leave. Ann, the mother of small children, immediately falls asleep on the sofa, only waking up when the conversation turns interesting or when the strawberry daiquiris are served. And I, well I pop out my contact lenses, put on these really ugly thick glasses, and start to chew gum. In other words, we all become our "real selves."

And the scary part is that our real selves aren't those highly successful superwomen we show to the outside world. No, our real selves are essentially 15-year-old junk-food-eating, giggling-at-boys, talking-about-sex teenage girls. I've come to realize that the point of this weekend is not female bonding or self-actualization, it's adolescent regression. Eat junk food, read trash, and talk until you fall asleep. It's a three-day slumber party.

I guess that's what also puts fear into the hearts and minds of our nearest and dearest. Most vulnerable to this paranoia are husbands and partners. Ann's husband, Don, is always the most worried. Weeks before each trip he begins to ask Ann on a regular basis, "So, ah, what do you guys talk about up there? Do you talk about guys...? About husbands...? About me?" The closer the trip gets, the more pitiful he becomes. He often tries to get in our good graces by buying us bottles of expensive wine for the trip, which we gladly take and then giggle when we see him, just to watch him squirm. This year our adolescent selves took over late one night and we called him and yelled into the phone, "Don, how could you?" It was almost like an anonymous phone call, but better. The gals also wrote a nice postcard to my present beau telling him that we were so happy to "know everything about him." We laughed for hours over that one.

If those poor men only knew – we really don't talk much about our present guys because we're too busy talking about past lovers or those we'd like to have. We laugh until we cry telling stories about jerks we once knew, and draw pictures of their anatomical parts. We decide who exactly would make Kevin Costner more happy, me or Becky. Every male model in every magazine is physically dissected for his sexual potential. We also check out the butt of the pizza delivery boy and pretend he isn't young enough to be one of our sons.

Mostly we sit in one place and eat, drink and talk. This is a typical conversation:

Ann: "So I told my mom that I really didn't feel that way..."

Kathy: "Yeah, I know what you mean. Do you like my hair color this year?"

Becky: "It's sort of M&M brown, isn't it? My mother says the same stuff to me. Jeez, I want a pizza..."

Maxine: "Then I said to my boss... sure, no eggplant. I like it more than last year. Why is it clip-ons hurt so much but look so great?"

Ann: "I do too. It's OK. Do you believe it?"

And the strange thing is that everyone understands the various strands of this three-day marathon conversation. If a topic or story is lost in the shuffle on, say, Friday night and not picked up until Sunday morning, no problem. And even more strange, all the stories eventually get finished before the weekend is over, and I bet any one of us could repeat every conversation word for word.

When the weekend's over we start the traditional round of complaints that sum up our failure at a meaningful experience: Like how come we never left the house except to go to the store? And maybe we should have looked out the window just once, forchristsake. Are we so shallow and unsophisticated that we polished off the chocolate chip cookie dough but left a full bottle of French wine? And hey, didn't someone have a life-crisis problem that we forgot to discuss? Maybe next year.

Once again we've shown that real sisterhood isn't exactly a group of mutually supportive women concerned with the welfare of their kind. No, it's more like a bunch of dames in bathrobes throwing back M&Ms and making each other laugh.

Last Laughs

"I hope the earthlings have adopted a more hospitable greeting since the last time we were here."

I SLEPT LIKE A BABY LAST NIGHT... EVERY COUPLE OF HOURS I WOKE UP SCREAMING

©1994 Soderblom

©1993 Phillip Jewell 9/6

TOMB OF THE UNKNOWN BUREAUCRAT

I MISS THE WOLF.

RIP

RIP

MUELLER

Credits